The
Railways
of
Harrogate and District

James Rogers

NORTH EASTERN RAILWAY ASSOCIATION

Published by the North Eastern Railway Association May 2000

ISBN 1 873513 33 X

Text & illustrations prepared by David & Claire Williamson

Printed by Cornbrook Precision Colour

THE NORTH EASTERN RAILWAY ASSOCIATION

The N.E.R.A. was formed in 1961 to cater for all those interested in the railways of the North East, in particular the North Eastern Railway and the Hull & Barnsley Railway, from their early history and development through to their working as part of the LNER, BR and post privatisation networks. This extends to also include the many independent and industrial railways that operated alongside the main line system. Interests cover all aspects of operations from locomotives, rolling stock, train services, architecture, signalling, shipping, road vehicles and staff matters – both for the general enthusiast and model maker.

With in excess of 600 members, regular meetings are held in York, Darlington, Hull, Leeds and London. A programme of outdoor visits, tours and walks is also arranged. There is also an extensive source of information in the Association's library with its collection of books, historical records, photographs and drawings.

A high quality illustrated journal, THE NORTH EASTERN EXPRESS, is issued to members quarterly accompanied by drawing supplements. Over 150 issues of the EXPRESS have now appeared and comprehensive indices list its innumerable articles. The journal is accompanied by a newsletter with membership topics, details of forthcoming meetings and events in the north-east, book reviews and recent articles of interest.

The NERA also markets an extensive range of NER documents, including diagram books, timetables and other booklets from original NER material.

A Membership Prospectus can be obtained from the Membership Secretary :
Mr. T. Morrell, 8 Prunus Avenue, Kingston Road, Willerby, Hull, HU10 6PH.

A sales list of other N.E.R.A. publications can be obtained from the Sales Officer :
Mrs. C. E. Williamson, 31 Moreton Avenue, Stretford, Manchester, M32 8BP.
(PLEASE ENCLOSE A STAMPED ADDRESSED 9" X 4" ENVELOPE
WITH YOUR ENQUIRIES).

Front Cover
Un-named English Electric Deltic, No. 9006, brings the down 'Queen of Scots' Pullman across Ripon Viaduct over the River Ure. No. 9006 was later named 'Fife & Forfar Yeomanry' in December 1964. The Pullman consist is headed by brake second car No. 68 (built by Metro-Cammell in 1928 as a kitchen third but converted in 1961 to a brake second) followed by first class parlour car 'Raven' (also built by Metro-Cammell in 1960/1). Ripon viaduct over the River Ure was authorised in June 1867 at a cost of £1829-1s-11d to replace an original wooden structure. The viaduct was demolished in May 1972. Colour-Rail DE447.

Title Page (1)
NER Worsdell class Q, 4-4-0, No.1871 passes Harrogate South signalbox with a southbound train – note the chocolate and cream nameboard below the windows. This signal box opened in 1897 as part of the rebuilding works at the south end of the station. This wooden structure replaced a much taller box sited on the other side of Station Bridge. G. Pierson collection.

Contents

Abbreviations

ASLEF	Associated Society of Locomotive Engineers & Firemen
BR	British Railways/British Rail
BTC	British Transport Commission
DMU	Diesel Multiple Unit
E&WYJR	East & West Yorkshire Junction Railway
ECML	East Coast Main Line
GN of E	Great North of England Railway
GNR	Great Northern Railway
H&RJR	Harrogate & Ripon Junction Railway
HST	High Speed Train
Jct.	Junction
L&T	Leeds & Thirsk Railway
L&Y	Lancashire & Yorkshire Railway
LMS	London Midland & Scottish Railway
LNER	London & North Eastern Railway
LNR	Leeds Northern Railway
LNWR	London & North Western Railway
LNY&D	Leeds North Yorkshire & Durham Railway
MTL	Mersey Transport Limited
NER	North Eastern Railway
NUR	National Union of Railwaymen
NVLR	Nidd Valley Light Railway
YN&B	York Newcastle & Berwick Railway
YNMR	York & North Midland Railway

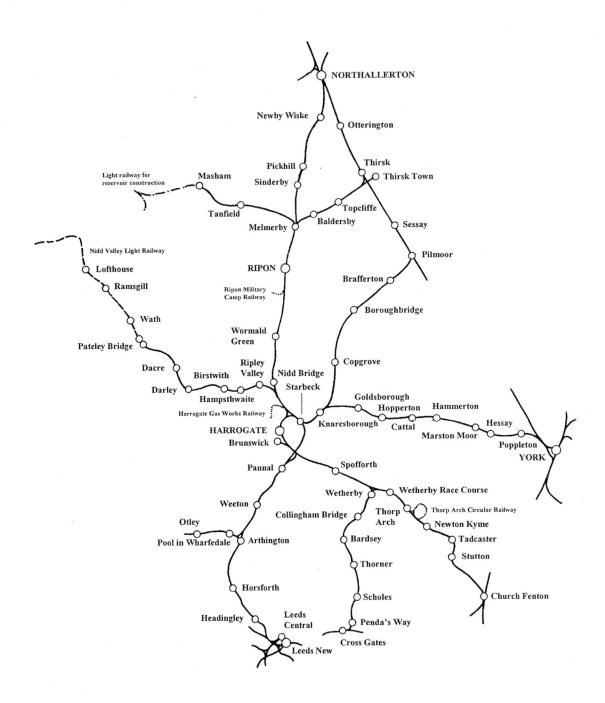

NORTHALLERTON

Newby Wiske

Otterington

Pickhill

Thirsk

Sinderby

Thirsk Town

Light railway for
reservoir construction

Masham

Tanfield

Topcliffe

Baldersby

Sessay

Melmerby

Nidd Valley Light Railway

Pilmoor

Lofthouse

RIPON

Brafferton

Ramsgill

Ripon Military
Camp Railway

Boroughbridge

Wath

Wormald
Green

Pateley Bridge

Copgrove

Dacre

Ripley
Valley

Birstwith

Nidd Bridge

Goldsborough

Darley

Starbeck

Hopperton

Hammerton

Hampsthwaite

Knaresborough

Cattal

Hessay

Harrogate Gas Works Railway

Marston Moor

HARROGATE

Poppleton

Brunswick

YORK

Pannal

Spofforth

Wetherby

Wetherby Race Course

Weeton

Collingham Bridge

Thorp
Arch

Thorp Arch Circular Railway

Otley

Newton Kyme

Pool in Wharfedale

Arthington

Bardsey

Tadcaster

Stutton

Horsforth

Thorner

Headingley

Leeds
Central

Scholes

Church Fenton

Penda's Way

Leeds New

Cross Gates

RAILWAYS OF HARROGATE & DISTRICT

Introduction

Today trains from Harrogate run mainly to Leeds or York. At one time it was very different. Harrogate was at the hub of a number of lines. Instead of travelling to York to catch a northbound train passengers could travel by a direct train via Ripon and Northallerton. Leeds bound passengers had a choice of two routes, the present one via Arthington, or one via Wetherby. In these days of congested roads it is worth remembering in 1963, the year of the Beeching Plan, trains from Harrogate travelled the 5 miles to Spofforth in only seven minutes, and the eight miles to Wetherby in only 12 minutes. Ripon, 11½ miles from Harrogate, was reached in only 14 minutes. There was at one time also through passenger trains to Bradford, Pateley Bridge, Thirsk, Boroughbridge and Pilmoor. Pilmoor was a remote station on the East Coast Main Line. It had no road access and its purpose was to allow passengers to change trains. Harrogate must be unique in that it once had a through passenger service which terminated less than 17 miles away at a point, Pilmoor, which most of the town's population have never heard of.

The Harrogate suburb of Starbeck owes its existence mainly to the goods train. For here a large marshalling yard, goods warehouse and locomotive shed were built. Work here was carried out 24 hours a day, yet today only the station and signal box remain, the goods trains have vanished from Harrogate's railways.

How all these lines came to be built and closed is told in the book. The book also tells the story of the people who worked and travelled on Harrogate's railways.

Acknowledgements

Much of the information contained in this book has been obtained from the "Leeds Mercury", the "Yorkshire Gazette", the Harrogate Herald", the Harrogate Advertiser" and other newspapers held at Leeds City Library, York City Library and Harrogate Library. Details of some accidents have been obtained from the official accident reports held at the National Railway Museum, York. The "Railway Times" newspaper has also been consulted at the NRM. Deposited plans, held at the West Yorkshire Record Office at Wakefield, have also been checked. Magazines consulted include the "Railway Magazine", "Railway World", "Trains Illustrated" and the "Railway Observer". The following books have also provided invaluable references: "North Eastern Locomotive Sheds" by Ken Hoole, "Titled Trains of Great Britain" by Cecil J. Allan and "Locomotive and Train Working in the latter Part of the 19th Century" by E.L. Ahrons. I would also like to thank the late Ken Hoole, A.N. MacKay, C.J. Woolstenholmes and other members of the North Eastern Railway Association for their help.

The drawings, plans and book layout for this publication have been prepared by David and Claire Williamson. They have also drawn on their own collections to source much of the photographic content. The publications team of the North Eastern Railway Association also wish to extend their thanks to the following individuals or organisations who have helped, offered ideas, loaned or allowed the use of historical documents and photographs in the course of the preparation of this publication: G. Pierson, J.F. Addyman, R.D. Pulleyn, J. Talbot, M. Grocock, J. Edgington, Pictorail, J. Peden, RAS Marketing, Colour-Rail, W. Fawcett, A. Cormack, S.Askew, M. Parkes, J. Armstrong (K.L. Taylor Collection), Ann Wilson - Curator of the Ken Hoole Study Centre at Darlington Railway Museum, Colin Foster and the Ken Hoole Trust, Alan Thompson and the J.W. Armstrong Trust.

Plate 1.1   The second Wetherby station was opened in 1902 after the line south to Leeds had been reconstructed to have double track. Beyond the platforms the lines to West and East Junctions went off to join the Harrogate and Church Fenton branch thus forming a triangular layout. There were horse and carriage loading dock sidings on both sides of the main station building seen here on the right. The original Y&NM station was sited just to the east of Wetherby East Junction.   Tom Smeaton/NERA Library.

Plate 1.2   Wooden scaffolding surrounds the piers of Crimple Viaduct as repairs take place to the structure c1906/7. To facilitate access a siding for the contractors was laid in at Follifoot signal box. This signal box was on the Leeds & Thirsk line, a short distance to the north of where this line passed beneath the York & North Midland viaduct. K. Hoole collection.

Chapter 1

THE

HARROGATE - CHURCH FENTON

AND

WETHERBY - LEEDS LINES

In 1841 the Great North of England Railway (GN of E) opened its main line from Darlington to York, where it joined the York & North Midland Railway (YNMR), which in turn joined the North Midland Railway's Derby - Leeds line near Normanton. This made a continuous line from Darlington to London, via York and Derby. In 1843 a group of Harrogate men proposed a railway from Bolton Percy, on the YNMR, to Harrogate. They estimated the railway would cost between £120,000 and £130,000 and have an annual income of £20,000. £12,000 from passenger traffic, £4,000 from coal, £3,000 from merchandise and £1,000 from agricultural produce, cattle etc. A survey was made by Joseph Locke, who had assisted Stephenson on the Liverpool & Manchester Railway. He suggested because of the steep approach to Harrogate the terminus should be at Starbeck, which being midway between Harrogate and Knaresborough, would serve both places. The promoters refused to build a branch from Starbeck to Harrogate but had no objection to local people doing so. This was not good enough for Knaresborough people who met in February 1844 to consider asking Parliament to compel the promoters to extend to Knaresborough. At this meeting mention was made of the Leeds & Thirsk Railway (L & T), proposed by Leeds businessmen, which would pass through Horsforth, Starbeck and Ripon before joining the GN of E near Thirsk. Although it would come no nearer Knaresborough than the Bolton Percy railway it would give the town access to both Leeds and the North, whereas the Bolton Percy Railway would run from nowhere to nowhere. It was therefore decided the L & T should have the town's fullest support. Three months later, when the Bolton Percy scheme went before Parliament, opposition from landowners ensured it was rejected. However it was taken up by the YNMR who obtained an Act on 21st July 1845 for a line from Church Fenton, on the YNMR, to Harrogate.

The YNMR's Church Fenton - Harrogate line was staked out in September 1845 and the following November tenders were sought for its construction. As first planned the line would have passed within yards of the Tewit Well and level crossings would have existed on Hookstone Road, and Leeds Road, near its junction with Otley Road. However the proposed route was later altered so the level crossings were eliminated and the line passed further away from the well. By April 1846 work had begun. In that month the local press reported that, to the astonishment of hundreds, men were working on the line on Sundays, and "surely such disgraceful proceedings would soon be stopped in Christian England." In September 1846 about 100 workmen struck work for a 6d a day rise. Armed with sticks they marched along the line throwing stones at those still at work until the constables arrived. After two days the men resumed work at the old rates and the ringleaders were sentenced to two months imprisonment with hard labour.

The influx of such a large workforce brought its problems. At Spofforth nine special constables were sworn in to help the regular force. Poaching and drunkenness became a problem. The "Harrogate Advertiser" reported in June 1847, that from time immemorial the area had been notorious for poaching but the offence had increased since the arrival of the navvies, despite numerous convictions. Neither the threat of fines nor the treadmill had any effect and every Sabbath bands of navvies could be seen in pursuit of game with indifference to the game laws and gamekeepers. One Sunday evening Policeman Young had met two stonemasons employed on the Church Fenton line loaded with hares and rabbits and on being questioned as to where they had bagged the game said they had purchased it, thus evading justice as the game laws gave no authority for detention on the highway.

On Follifoot Moor, where a tunnel was being dug to carry the Church Fenton line through Follifoot ridge, a shanty town was built to house the navvies. In June 1847 a stranger was jailed for having spent a night without permission in one of the huts. The same month a hawker attempting to ply his trade in the shanty town had his goods stolen by some drunken navvies.

The goods, with the exception of a packet of needles, were quickly returned when a constable was called.

In October 1847 an Irishman was discovered crawling along the road near Crimple with one leg bandaged. He said he had been working in the Follifoot tunnel for three days but had been dismissed without payment after sustaining an injury little better than a fracture of the leg. Fortunately he met a good Samaritan who generously contributed to his needs. The local press thought this a shameful piece of conduct on the part of those connected with the tunnel.

A navvy who had never been in a lock up before he came to Harrogate was jailed in June 1847 for being drunk and insulting Mrs Gordon of the Cheltenham Pump Rooms on her way to church. Another, known as Navvy Jack, was ordered to keep the peace for six months after making a great disturbance at Kirkby Overblow in October 1847. He had been drunk and, with others, had alarmed the whole neighbourhood by swearing violently with scarcely any clothes on.

Work on building the line could be dangerous. In June 1847 two labourers working in the stone quarry near Crimple Viaduct had a miraculous escape. A huge block of stone rolled onto them and every one expected them to be killed but on being removed from underneath the stone they were found to have suffered, as the "Harrogate Advertiser", put it, "little injury further than a severe crushing."

A man working Follifoot Tunnel had his skull fractured by a fall of earth and a labourer working in the deep cutting on the Oatlands Estate had a narrow escape from death by being knocked down by a stone which fell from a barrow he was conducting up a steep inclined plank. In July 1847 a Spofforth carpenter fell to his death in Haggs Cutting, near Spofforth whilst helping to dismantle a crane. The following May a navvy known as Lanky was killed by a fall of earth in the same cutting. In January 1848 a man employed on the Church Fenton line sustained a fractured jaw and other injuries through not having stood a safe distance when firing blasts in a cutting at Harrogate.

The line was opened between Church Fenton and Spofforth on 10th August 1847 with omnibuses running between Spofforth and Harrogate. In October 1847 financial considerations led to nine-tenths of the workmen being laid off for the winter. Despite this the last of the 31 arches in the Crimple Viaduct was keyed-in two months later, on 23rd December, but the following month part of the roof of Prospect Tunnel collapsed.

In June 1848 a man responsible for paying the wages of 150 workmen on the Church Fenton line absconded with the money. In an attempt to obtain some financial recompense the men refused to let some horses, previously owned by him, leave the yard of the "Castle Inn", Spofforth, where they were stabled. A serious disturbance was prevented by the arrival of special constables from Knaresborough and Wetherby.

The remaining part of the line, that between Spofforth and Harrogate, was suddenly and unceremoniously opened on 20th July 1848. The first timetable showed departures from Harrogate at 7.00 am, 9.15 am, 12 noon, 2.30 pm and 6.00 pm and arrivals at 9.30 am, 11.45 am, 2.15 pm, 4.55 pm and 7.58 pm. Trains, which took on average 50 minutes to run the 18½ miles,

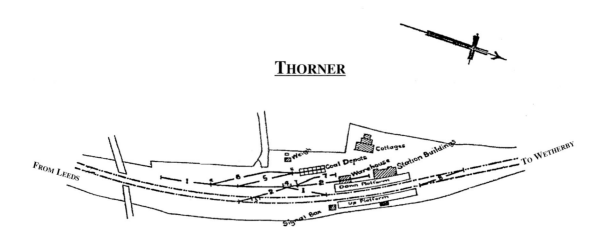

THORNER

D.E.Y. 16.12.1912

were frequently late, causing the "Harrogate Advertiser" to suggest in September 1848 that either the trains be made to conform to the timetable or the timetable be made to conform to the trains. One passenger later suggested because there was often a long wait at Church Fenton for an onward train a reading room ought to be provided there.

In 1850 a Spofforth man was charged with riding from Leeds to Spofforth without paying his fare. At Leeds a friend had given him a return ticket to Spofforth which was not transferable. In his defence he stated he had not intended to defraud the railway company and on learning he had committed an offence had offered to pay the 2s 6d fare. The court dismissed the case when it learnt the railway by-laws had not been exhibited at Spofforth station as required by law.

The L & T opened its line from Leeds to Thirsk, via Starbeck, throughout in 1849 and in 1851 a line was opened between Starbeck and York. With direct trains to both Leeds and York available by these routes the Church Fenton line suffered. By 1853 trains had been reduced to three a day in each direction. Departures from Harrogate were at 9.00 am, 2.40 pm and 6.00 pm while trains arrived in Harrogate at 12 noon, 5.40 pm and 8.00 pm. Trains approached Harrogate station, called Brunswick, after a nearby Hotel, through a tunnel 286 yards long. The station was a temporary wooden structure with some buildings converted from farm buildings that had occupied the site before the railway came. In 1853 there appears to have been no watering facilities for locomotives there for a passenger asked that year if it was necessary for trains to stop for water at Prospect Tunnel so soon after leaving Harrogate.

At least two accidents occurred at Brunswick station. In March 1859 a porter was killed when crushed between the buffers of two wagons. He was very much respected as a civil and obliging man at the station. In June the same year the 11.50 am from Church Fenton emerged from the tunnel and was climbing the incline into the station when a horse box became derailed and in turn derailed a third class carriage. Although the buffers of the horsebox penetrated the carriage no one was hurt.

During its short existence the station had at least three different stationmasters. In 1854 a passenger placed a scarf on a carriage seat to reserve it for a friend. Another passenger complained it was preventing him taking the seat and the stationmaster ordered its removal. This caused the first passenger to complain that the stationmaster was "a low fellow ignorant of his duties and altogether unfit for his situation", and added that it had surprised many that the directors had given such a man the job. The stationmaster in 1857 was a Mr Gowling who had been a captain in the 72nd Highlanders. He died that year after being taken ill during a service in St John's Church. In 1855 the booking clerk at Brunswick was arrested for embezzlement.

The stationmaster at Tadcaster was also the subject of complaint. On Whit Monday 1857 a woman with three children aged two, four and seven went to Tadcaster station. The stationmaster, Mr Laytham, issued her with a third class ticket and a half fare ticket for the eldest child. Shortly afterwards she discovered she was 3d short in her change and after some argument the stationmaster gave her the 3d. Half an hour later, as the train approached, the stationmaster asked if she had a ticket for the child aged four. She replied he knew she had not, he had seen all the

COLLINGHAM BRIDGE

Plate 1.3   WD 2-8-0, No. 90461 passes through Thorpe Arch station with a class H down freight from Teeside to the West Riding comprised of mainly steel carrying wagons. With the construction of the Royal Ordinance Factory the station platforms were extended to cope with longer workmens trains. In the up goods yard an old gunpowder van serves as a goods store. J.W. Armstrong Trust.

Plate 1.4   An ex LMS Fowler 2-6-4T, No. 42409 passes Spofforth signal box with an RCTS railtour special from Leeds in October 1963. The signal box was designed with one corner chamfered to clear the main Harrogate – Wetherby road which crossed the railway at this point. D.J. Williamson collection.

Plate 1.5   Looking south from Crimple Viaduct towards Prospect Tunnel the tracks to the right formed the Pannal Loop. This loop was part of the 1862 improvements in the Harrogate area and joined the Harrogate - Church Fenton line to the Leeds Northern line at Pannal Junction. Prospect Tunnel was 825 yards long. The signal box seen on the left, opened in November 1902, replaced an earlier box nearer to the viaduct.   K. Hoole collection.

children when she bought the tickets and had not told her she needed one. The stationmaster then said he would not allow her to board the train, even though she offered to pay for the child. After the train had gone she asked for a refund but the stationmaster refused and told her to go about her business. She then had to walk four miles on a sultry day to Bolton Percy, where she caught a train to York. When informed of the day's events her husband took a day off work, without pay, and walked to York to complain to the railway authorities. He received a refund of his wife's fare from Tadcaster to Bolton Percy, a free third class ticket for himself back to Tadcaster, and a promise his complaint would be looked into. He later complained this promise was not kept.

In 1854 the railways running into Harrogate amalgamated to form the North Eastern Railway (NER). This company linked the L & T to the Church Fenton line by a new line from Pannal Jct. to Crimple Jct. A new line was also built through central Harrogate where a new station was constructed. From here trains continued north to rejoin the L & T at Bilton or Starbeck. These new lines and station opened on 1st August 1862. Brunswick station then closed to passengers but remained open for goods traffic until about 1864, after which it was demolished. No detailed plans, drawings or photographs are known to exist of it. A plaque marking its site was unveiled by the Mayor of Harrogate on 20th December 1949. The tunnel leading to Brunswick station was also abandoned and in 1938 was converted into an air raid shelter capable of sheltering 5,000 people.

In 1865 a new company, the Leeds North Yorkshire & Durham Railway (LNY&D), proposed a line from Leeds to Stockton, via Wetherby and Easingwold, with a number of branches, including one to Scarborough. To counter this the NER obtained powers on 23rd June 1866 for a line from Cross Gates to Wetherby, and one from Knaresborough to Boroughbridge, which, with existing lines and new loops, would form a new route from Leeds to Scarborough. Unfortunately the LNY&D proposal was rejected by Parliament because the costs of construction had been underestimated and soon after the NER bought out the leading promoters. With the would be competitor gone the NER sought powers to abandon their Wetherby and Boroughbridge schemes but were opposed by Wetherby and Boroughbridge. The NER therefore agreed to build the Wetherby and Boroughbridge lines but obtained powers in August 1869 which allowed them extra time to do so. Tenders to construct the Cross Gates - Wetherby line were sought in November 1871 and the line, which was single track, opened on 1st May 1876. The junction with the Harrogate - Church Fenton line faced Church Fenton which meant trains between Harrogate and Leeds had to reverse at Wetherby. The previous November the "Yorkshire Gazette" had reported the platforms at Wetherby had been raised so there was no longer the steep and dangerous descent from carriages and the "miserable little shed" which acted as a waiting room on the down side had been pulled down, but it remained to see what would be put in its place. The first timetable showed four trains in each direction on weekdays but there were complaints that the first train, which arrived in Leeds at 9.40 am, arrived too late for businessmen. It was also thought 5.30 pm was too early for the last train to leave Leeds for Wetherby.

The Cross Gates - Wetherby line was doubled in 1901 and, to enable trains between Harrogate and Leeds to use the route without reversal, a new south-west curve was built at Wetherby, together with a new station. The old station was thereafter used for goods only. From 1st October 1901 five express trains a day in each direction between Harrogate and Leeds were transferred from the Arthington to the Wetherby route, although the new Wetherby station was not opened until 1st July 1902. Congestion at Holbeck was avoided but Harrogate passengers complained connections there were now lost. On 3rd December 1901 one of these trains, the 4.32 pm Leeds - Newcastle express, hauled by Class R, 4-4-0, No. 2109, was derailed on a curve near Bardsey station when the tender and all six vehicles left the rails. The tender became detached from the train, was dragged forward by the engine, but rerailed itself on a crossover before coming to rest 150 yards from the rest of the train. The first four vehicles remained more or less upright in the six foot. The fifth was completely derailed, partly in the six foot and partly in the four foot, while the sixth came to rest across the down line with its rear bogie still on the rails. Seventeen passengers were injured but none seriously.

Stutton station closed to passengers on 1st July 1905. It was about half a mile from Tadcaster station and the number of passengers did not justify two stations so close together. After closure the down side waiting room was let to the parish council for their meetings.

In April 1911 a large crowd, returning from the races, made a dash for a Bradford train at Wetherby station before it had stopped, with the result a passenger was pushed off the platform and killed. The relief stationmaster had a staff of 11 to assist him but that day they were unable to hold back the hundreds of people on the platform.

A new station to serve Wetherby Racecourse was opened in 1924. This station was last used on Whit Monday 18th May 1959 and demolished in 1962. Race trains however continued to run, but passengers had to use Wetherby's main station.

Another new station, Penda's Way, was opened in 1939. It was built to serve a new housing estate and consisted of station buildings and two platforms, each 120 yards long, linked by a footbridge. Not including site clearance, and the laying of foundations, the station was built and painted in a day. Work began at 10.00 am on Saturday 3rd June and was finished by 6.00 pm the following evening. The station opened on 5th June 1939, the first ticket being ceremoniously issued to the Lord Mayor of Leeds.

Life on the Wetherby lines was not without incident. On 27th December 1853 a railway man was severely injured when a Harrogate bound goods train was derailed in Prospect Tunnel. Shortly after the 6 30 pm train passed through Spofforth on Boxing Day 1867 two boys told the station master an accident had occurred. He hurried down the line and found Thomas Petty, the porter and gatekeeper, lying in a pool of blood. Further down the line he found retired book-keeper James Webster, dead on the line. On regaining consciousness Petty said he had seen Webster crossing the line and had told him not to do so as a train was coming, but he had paid

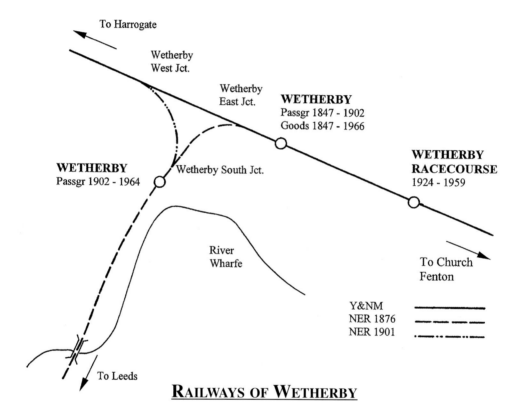

RAILWAYS OF WETHERBY

no attention. Petty tried to drag Webster away but he was determined to be over the line and was very impertinent. As they struggled the train knocked them down. At the inquest the jury returned a verdict of accidental death, and expressed their strong opinion that, because of the considerable amount of traffic at Spofforth, the gate keeper ought to be constantly there to attend the gates. Also additional lights ought to be provided at the crossing.

In 1902 Wetherby Rural District Council passed a resolution to the effect 'that in view of the heavy amount of road traffic over the level crossing at Spofforth, and the great number of express and other trains passing trough the station, that the NER have their attention drawn to the danger to human life which was involved and take immediate steps to remedy the danger'. What exactly the danger was, was not stated.

In 1870 a Harrogate bound passenger train ran into two chains and a stone placed on the line near Wetherby. Fortunately the train was travelling slowly and no derailment occurred.

A tin box, addressed to a Miss Wood, William Street, Tadcaster, arrived at Tadcaster station from Rochdale in 1871. Because there was no such address it was kept until called for but soon began to smell. On its being opened it was found to contain a child's body.

The lamp room and adjoining passenger shed at Thorpe Arch station were destroyed by fire

Plate 1.6 Wetherby Racecourse station opened in 1924 about one mile east of the town. NER Class S, 4-6-0, No. 743 stands at the station with a race special (complete with reporting board no. 126). The station, opened on race days only, was last used in March 1959. LNER/K. Hoole collection.

Plate 1.7 Southern Railway 'Schools' class, 4-4-0, No. 30925 'Cheltenham'and Midland Railway class 2P, 4-4-0, No. 40646, double head the RCTS 'East Midlander' special past Wetherby South signal box on 13th May 1962. This train which had started from Nottingham Victoria ran via Church Fenton to Wetherby where the engines ran round. The special then ran tender first through Harrogate to Starbeck where it reversed again and then continued past Ripon to Darlington. The reversal in Wetherby was enforced because the direct East to West Junction line had been severed in December 1961. G. Pierson collection.

Plate 1.8 English Electric Type 3 No. 6736 (later class 37 No.37067) passes Scholes station on a steel train. Note the diesel brake tender behind the engine to provide extra braking effort on what was probably a largely unfitted train. D.J. Williamson collection.

in December 1874 when firewood placed in front of a fire to dry caught fire. In July 1926 the Spofforth station master found a ten year old boy, who had fallen from a train, walking on the line, dazed but suffering little more than cuts and bruises.

A police constable committed suicide in August 1933 by jumping from the 9.30 am Leeds - Harrogate train as it passed through Prospect Tunnel.

The "Northern Belle" a luxury train, intended to take passengers on a "land cruise" was introduced in 1933. Its itinerary varied each year and in 1934 Harrogate was included. The train, hauled by Class A1 Pacific, No.2546, "Donovan", left Kings Cross at 9.30 pm on 1st June for Wetherby. After an overnight stop two Class K3, 2-6-0s, worked the train to Harrogate where passengers were taken on a motor tour of the district. They then rejoined the train at Ripon and proceeded to Barnard Castle behind another K3, No. 17. The "Northern Belle" was withdrawn on the outbreak of war.

In April 1942, during the Second World War, the Thorpe Arch circular railway was opened to serve an ammunition factory whose buildings were spread over a wide area to minimise the effects of any explosion. Trains gained access to the railway from the Church Fenton line near Thorpe Arch station and proceeded in a clockwise direction around the 6½ miles of single track, which was equipped with automatic colour light signalling in order that several trains could go round at once. After depositing passengers at the four stations, Walton, Roman Road, Ranges and River, the trains would wait until shifts changed then go round again picking up the outgoing workers. Workmen's trains continued to use the railway after the war but ceased on 15th August 1958.

In 1902 the Great Northern Railway began running through trains between Kings Cross and Harrogate, via Church Fenton and Spofforth and in the mid 1920s the "Harrogate Pullman" took this route on its non-stop run between Kings Cross and Harrogate. Harrogate – London trains ceased to use the Church Fenton line in March 1947 but on 2nd October 1956, after a crane, being used on maintenance work, was derailed in Bramhope Tunnel, the up "Yorkshire Pullman" was diverted via Spofforth and Church Fenton and did not call at Leeds. Other trains were diverted via Wetherby and some replaced by buses.

In summer 1950 of the nine passenger trains from Wetherby to Leeds, Mondays to Fridays, one started from Wetherby, five from Harrogate, two from Selby and one from Church Fenton. There was also one Harrogate - Wetherby train. On Saturdays two additional Harrogate - Wetherby – Leeds trains were run, as well as a Newcastle - Leeds - Birmingham train, which ran via Harrogate and Wetherby but did not stop at either place. In the opposite direction, Mondays to Fridays, there was a Llandudno - Newcastle express which called at Wetherby at 8.12 pm, five Leeds - Wetherby - Harrogate trains, one of which continued to Northallerton, and one Wetherby - Harrogate train. There were also two trains from Leeds to Selby, via Wetherby and Church Fenton, one of which continued to Bridlington, via Market Weighton. On Saturdays there were two extra Leeds - Wetherby – Harrogate trains. There was no Sunday service and no through trains between Harrogate and Church Fenton.

NEWTON KYME

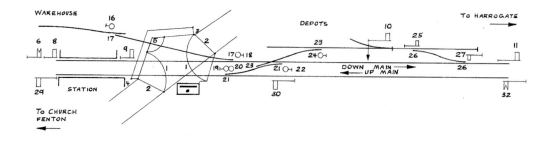

No. of Levers : 32
Spares : 7, 12 - 15, 28, 31.
No. 1 : Gatewheel
No. 5 : Gatelock – Down Siding.

Reference : N.E.R. Engineers Office, York,
DRG. No. S13/98/2 dated 16·5·1907.
P.R.O. MT6 1647/2.

Landslips plagued the Leeds - Wetherby line. In 1877 the line was blocked by a landslip near Thorner but a service was maintained by trains running to either side of the blockage and passengers walking the intervening distance. On 2nd December 1907 slips occurred between Bardsey and Thorner and stopped all traffic for 19 days. From 18th February 1953 the down line rear Bardsey was closed for 12 days after about 70 yards of embankment subsided and left it suspended.

The Wetherby lines were used by goods trains between Teesside and the West Riding, especially during and after the Second World War when such trains were transferred from the Arthington route. On 23rd January 1913 the 11.30 pm Starbeck - Gascoigne Wood coal train became divided on restarting from Crimple and arrived at Spofforth with only 52 wagons. It was held until Class 290, 0-6-0T, No. 166, which had assisted the train to Crimple arrived with the remaining 14 wagons and guard's van. The same thing happened to the same train on 21st June 1915, Class P3, 0-6-0, No. 1044 arrived at Spofforth with only 47 wagons. The remaining 12 were brought forward by assisting loco, Class Y 4-6-2T No. 1126. Seven wagons and a guard's van that ran away from the 10.50 am Milford - Stockton goods on 14th November 1947 were derailed by catch points between Spofforth and Crimple. The rest of the train was stopped after the Crimple signalman noticed it pass without a guard's van. On 29th November 1948 the 9.55 pm Neville Hill - Stockton goods arrived at Crimple with only two wagons out of 50 still attached to the locos, Class J21, 0-6-0, No. 5036 and WD 2-8-0, No. 77003. One of these wagons was derailed and had shed its load of timber onto the line near Spofforth. The other wagons had become detached between Wetherby and Spofforth. On 8th October 1957 eight wagons and a guard's van were derailed by catch points between Spofforth and Crimple after breaking away from a Normanton – Newport goods. Through goods trains between Teesside and the West Riding ceased to use the line in September 1959 when they were transferred to the East Coast Main line. By December 1961 through running between Harrogate and Church Fenton, without reversal at Wetherby, was impossible because the line between Wetherby West and East junctions had been partially lifted.

As an economy measure the night shift was withdrawn from signal boxes on the Leeds - Harrogate, via Arthington, route in 1959. As a consequence the 3.57 am Leeds - Ripon, the 5.50 am Leeds -Thirsk and the 10.50 pm Leeds - Harrogate were transferred to the Wetherby route, although they did not call at any of its stations. With the dieselisation of the Liverpool - Newcastle (via Harrogate) expresses the need to change engines at Leeds was eliminated. To avoid reversal at Leeds these trains, of which there were two in each direction, were on weekdays from 2nd January 1961 re-routed to run via Wetherby, instead of Arthington. On Sundays there were two expresses using the Leeds Northern line, one from Manchester to Newcastle, and one from Newcastle to Liverpool. These continued to travel via Arthington.

In January 1964 there were, Mondays to Fridays, six trains from Wetherby to Leeds. Of these three started from Wetherby, two from Harrogate and one, at 7.44 am, from Church Fenton, but there was no return service over the Wetherby - Church Fenton line. On Saturdays there were two extra Harrogate - Wetherby trains but two less Wetherby - Leeds trains. In the opposite direction, Mondays to Fridays, there were four trains from Leeds to Wetherby, only one of which continued to Harrogate. On Saturdays there were five trains from Leeds to Wetherby, one terminated at Wetherby, but three continued to Harrogate, and one to Northallerton. There were also two trains in each direction between Liverpool and Newcastle which ran non-stop between Leeds and Harrogate. Also the trains from Leeds at 3.57 am to Ripon and 6.05 am to Northallerton ran non-stop to Harrogate. There was no Sunday service. The first train of the day to call at Wetherby was the 6.39 am from Harrogate, which departed at 6.53 am and arrived in Leeds at 7.23 am. The last was, Mondays to Fridays, the 5.35 pm from Leeds which departed Wetherby at 6.11 pm and arrived in Harrogate at 6.30 pm. On Saturdays the last train was the 6.13 pm from Harrogate which left Wetherby for Leeds at 6.27 pm.

Passenger services were withdrawn from the Harrogate - Church Fenton and Wetherby - Leeds lines from 6th January 1964 and the line between Crimple Jct. and Wetherby South Jct. closed completely. Local goods trains continued to use the Leeds - Wetherby – Church Fenton line, although after 6th January 1964 the only intermediate stations open for goods were Scholes, Wetherby, Thorpe Arch, Tadcaster and Stutton. By the end of the year only Wetherby and Tadcaster remained. Goods traffic was withdrawn from these stations on 4th April 1966 and 30th November 1966 respectively.

Plate 2.1   Unlike the castellated north portal of Bramhope Tunnel the southern end was much plainer but had substantial retaining walls to the cutting sides. The tunnel was some 2 miles, 241 yards long - the eighth longest in the UK. Built between 1845 and 1849 on a gradient of 1 in 94 falling towards Arthington the tunnel was cut through shale and sandstone. The contractor, Thomas Bray, had to contend with an enormous influx of some 1,563,480,000 gallons of water whilst it was under construction.   Ken Hoole collection.

Plate 2.2   Taken from Arthington South signal box at the southern apex of the triangular junction, the Otley branch, which opened on 1st February 1865, is shown swinging sharply off to the left from the Leeds and Thirsk line.   Looking along the main line Arthington North signal box can be seen. This station had four platforms, the main passenger buildings, of 1895, being situated in the vee of the junction. There were never any platforms on the north to west curve.   Arthington station closed on 22nd March 1965 together with the Otley branch.   Tom Smeaton/NERA Library.

Plate 2.3   The embankment at Weeton meant the platforms and some of the buildings were of lightweight construction. Exceptions were the waiting rooms on the right hand up Leeds platform and the signal box seen beyond the platform end. In the background private owner coal wagons stand to the right of the hipped roof wooden goods shed in this 1920's view. Weeton had been the temporary terminus of the line, when on 1st September 1848, the railway opened for business between Wormald Green and Weeton.   D.J. Williamson collection.

Chapter 2

THE LEEDS NORTHERN LINE

When planning their main line south in 1834 the GN of E had considered dividing it at Sessay, one line going to York, the other to Leeds, but only the York line was built, that to Leeds being considered impracticable because of the hilly ground between Harrogate and Leeds. When the L & T was proposed the GN of E feared the new line would become a competitor and to win over some of the L & Ts supporters announced plans for a line from Pilmoor, on the Darlington - York line, to Knaresborough and Harrogate, via Boroughbridge. From this line a branch would run to Ripon. This Harrogate & Ripon Junction Railway (H&RJR) would in reality have only skirted Knaresborough and its terminus would have been at Collins Cottage, a remote spot on the Wetherby Road, two miles south-east of Harrogate. The L & T promoters only wanted a more direct linc to the Tees and suggested to the GN of E they become partners in a joint venture. The GN of E rejected this because they thought that even if the L & T could be built the working of it afterwards would be difficult. Later the GN of E suggested the L & T build only that part of the line between Leeds and Collins Cottage, where the H & RJR could be joined. This was rejected because the L & T considered they would have to build the most difficult part of the line for the least financial reward. The GN of E next proposed the L & T abandon their plan completely and in return the H & RJR would be extended to Leeds, via Wetherby. This meant the L & T giving up the route they felt best suited their needs. They therefore rejected it, but the GN of E announced they would extend to Leeds nevertheless.

Knaresborough residents met to discuss both schemes on 19th December 1844. The L & T plans now included a branch from Starbeck to Knaresborough, but the GN of E claimed this would mean Knaresborough would be at the end of a branch on which would be a gradient of 1 in 103, too steep for passenger trains. Gradients on the main line would also be too steep and, with the many curves, make the line uneconomical to work and a nuisance. The L & T accused the GN of E of exaggerating the gradients and doubted they would extend to Leeds if the L & T was abandoned. A signpost might then be erected at Pilmoor reading "Harrogate and Knaresborough, No Thoroughfare." The L & T would link Knaresborough with both the North and the South and bring coal to the town at 6s 8d a ton, or less. The GN of E charged 12s a ton at Thirsk and they would not bring it the greater distance to Knaresborough for less. After some further discussion the meeting pledged its support to the L & T.

When the L & T went before Parliament the GN of E provided the main opposition until suddenly they announced they had abandoned their H & RJR scheme and withdrew their opposition. This was on the orders of George Hudson, the YNMR Chairman, who had gained control of the GN of E. Other minor opposition was overcome and the Act authorising the building of the L & T received the Royal Assent on 21st July 1845.

To reach Teesside the L & T at first intended to use other companies' lines north of Thirsk but soon felt it desirable to have their own line throughout. They therefore proposed a line from Melmerby, on the original Leeds - Thirsk line, to Stockton, via Northallerton. Opposition from landowners, and George Hudson, led them to abandon the Melmerby-Northallerton section and on 16th July 1846 they obtained an Act authorising a line from Northallerton to Billingham. Between Thirsk and Northallerton the main York – Newcastle line was to be used. The L & T however were determined to be independent and on 22nd July 1848 finally obtained powers to build the Melmerby - Northallerton section. Consideration was given to building the L & T as an atmospheric railway but its promoters had second thoughts and gave their engineer permission to build only the Knaresborough branch, and a proposed Harrogate branch, as such before completely abandoning the idea.

In order to build the L & T it was divided into six contracts and let as follows: -

The Leeds, from Leeds to Horsforth, to James Bray on 10th October 1845
The Bramhope, from Horsforth to Weeton, to James Bray on 1st October 1845
The Pannal, from Weeton to Starbeck, to James Bray on 2nd April 1846
The Nidd, from Starbeck to Wormald Green, to Mark Faviell & Son on 1st October 1846
The Ripon, from Wormald Green to Ripon, to Richard Duckett on 19th November 1846
The Thirsk, from Ripon to Thirsk, to Richard Duckett on 13th August 1846

Work began on 20th October 1845 with the digging of the No 1 airshaft of the Bramhope Tunnel. Other shafts were sunk later. By this means a number of faces could be at work simultaneously, but it was not until 27th November 1848 that a clear path was made through the tunnel. The work almost bankrupted the company. No less than 1,563,480,000 gallons of water had to be pumped out, and at the tunnel's south end the nature of the soil meant several hundred yards had to be added and retaining walls built to hold back the cutting sides. This made the tunnel's final length 2 miles and 241 yards. The first train through on 31st May 1849, hauled by the contractor's locomotive "Stephenson", carried L & T officials from Arthington. To commemorate those who died building the tunnel a memorial in the shape of the tunnel's northern portal was erected in the churchyard at Otley.

On 30th March 1846 a procession with bands playing and flags flying marched from Pool to witness the laying of the foundation stone of the Wharfe Viaduct. Under the stone were placed a newspaper, some coins, a map of the line and a copy of the L & T Act. The L & T Chairman, who laid the stone, was presented with a commemorative trowel and mallet whilst the workmen were given a day's holiday and free ale. On 19th October 1847 the seventh arch collapsed into the river killing two workmen. No other part of the structure was affected and by February 1849 the contractor was running his locomotive over the viaduct, the last stone having been laid on 30th November 1848.

The line between Thirsk and Ripon was opened for goods traffic on 5th January 1848. Permission for the line to be used for passenger traffic was refused until the cutting north of Ripon station was finished, the line through it correctly laid, and two bridges, one over the Swale, the other at Hutton Conyers, strengthened. This was done and on 31st May 1848 a train left Thirsk at 9.00 am carrying Thirsk people to Ripon. It returned at 10.30 am with over 500 Ripon citizens and two musical bands. Two further journeys were made about 6.00 pm to return the passengers home and the following day the line opened to the public, with four trains in each direction a day, except Sundays when there were two. The site of Ripon station was considered temporary. A better site existed nearer the city centre, where the line was to cross the canal, but the directors needed an early profit and as the line then came no nearer Ripon than the North Bridge that is where the station was built. At Ripon a wooden viaduct was built over the Ure. The embankment south of this was prone to subsidence and presented the contractor with many problems. Soil from a cutting north of Ripon station was used in its formation but was insufficient and a further supply had to be obtained by purchasing topsoil from nearby fields. In one of these an ancient human skeleton was found. Human remains were also found at Bilton when navvies uncovered a flat stone under which was a jar containing bones. These were later displayed at the nearby "Gardener's Arms" public house.

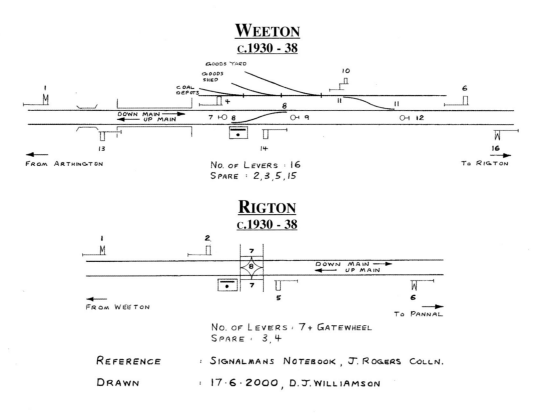

18

Three men and a boy were severely injured on 3rd February 1848 when part of a wooden framework collapsed during construction of a bridge over the Skell at Ripon. In April 1848 a sub-contractor, making the line across Monkton Moor, was fined £5 for selling beer without a licence. In his defence he said he had to supply beer to his men to keep them at work. Two years earlier at Wescoe Hill, near Weeton, there had been a fight involving many drunken navvies.

An Act had been obtained on 9th July 1847 to deviate the line in the Crimple Valley so it passed west of Collins Cottage instead of east, thus shortening the line by about half a mile. During construction of a bridge to carry the Harrogate - Wetherby road over the deviation complaints were made that building materials on the road meant carriages could not pass each other for some distance. In 1847 floods swept away the coffer dam built to assist the building of the Nidd Viaduct near Ripley. This setback was overcome and on 24th May 1848 the last arch in the viaduct was closed. Faviell, the contractor, who received a silver trowel to commemorate the event, felt gratified that during the viaduct's construction no accidents had occurred. A band played lively tunes but rain made most people glad to leave the ceremony. Faviell later entertained friends to dinner at "Gascoigne's Hotel" (now the "County") in Harrogate while his men were given a day's holiday and a free supper at the "Ship Inn". The officiating mason wished the viaduct would stand forever and the local press had little doubt it would stand for centuries as proof of what human strength could do. Five days later the last of the 10 arches in the L & Ts Crimple Viaduct was closed.

The report of the L & T directors in February 1849 states the line between Ripon and Weeton opened on 13th September 1848. However the "Harrogate Advertiser" of 16th September 1848 reported the line between Starbeck and Ripon was opened on Thursday 14th September 1848 and "with the exception of a few unintelligible posters issued at a late hour no announcement of the event was made. Even when it became known the line would open on Thursday nothing was definitely known of the intended arrangements; so much for the pomp and circumstance of such events in this part of the country. Several trains ran throughout the day and many people made a first trip to Ripon by rail. Some of the more rustic inhabitants seemed to regard each approaching train as a monster of the most remarkable character, cows, pigs and sheep, to whose ears the loud snorting of the steam courser was peculiarly foreign, darted off at the first rumbling sound as though a whole garrison of butchers, knives in hand, was following at their heels".

By February 1849 the Pannal contract was being worked as a single line, the other line being used far conveying ballast and completing the cutting at Rigton. The only stations built on a permanent basis were those at Thirsk, Topcliffe and Starbeck. The others were temporary wooden structures meant to remain until traffic developed.

Originally it was intended the railway would cross the Aire Valley, near Leeds, on an embankment but a viaduct was substituted. The last arch in this viaduct was keyed-in on 23rd March 1849 and on 9th July 1849 the final section of the L & T was opened between Weeton and Leeds. Special trains ran from Leeds to Thirsk where an informal dinner was held in the carriage shed. The next day the line was opened to the public with five passenger trains in each direction each weekday, except Tuesdays and Saturdays, when there was an additional train from Thirsk.

The coming of the railways spelled the end for the stagecoaches. A railway passenger noted in July 1849, when crossing the Great North Road between Melmerby and Baldersby, that the

PANNAL

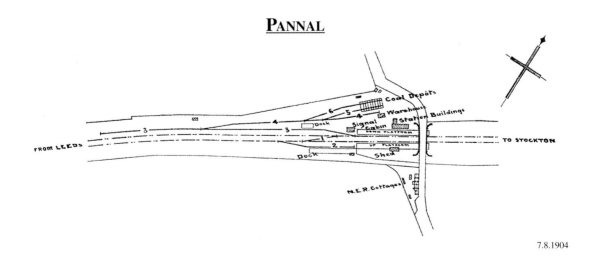

7.8.1904

19

Plate 2.4 *Pannal station situated between the main Leeds road at Spacey Houses and Pannal village had three goods sidings off a headshunt on the down side plus a loading dock on the up side. Seen here in 1958, Pannal retained its signal box and lattice post signals until March 1969. Goods facilities had already been withdrawn four years previously. Today the station remains open; the station building is now a public house.*
D.J. Williamson collection.

Plate 2.5   *LNER class D49 4-4-0, No. 72763, 'The Fitzwilliam' takes the Harrogate line at Bilton Junction with an up local train comprised of Gresley teak panelled and BR standard Mark 1coaches. The Leeds and Thirsk line runs off to the right of the engine towards Starbeck.*
D.J. Williamson collection.

famous coaching inn the "Red House", where over 1,000 horses had been stabled and where grooms, ostlers and waiters had been ceaselessly occupied, was now deserted and overgrown. The "Telegraph" coach which had run between Harrogate and Ripon for 70 years ceased to run on the opening of the Starbeck - Ripon section of line. Another "Telegraph", which ran between Leeds and Harrogate, and the "Union", which ran between Knaresborough and Leeds, both ceased to run on the opening throughout of the L & T.

The L & T proved less profitable than anticipated. In September 1850 a committee appointed to look into the line's management reported, of the lime made at Wormald Green station none was sold in the vicinity, and at Starbeck there was no agent to solicit traffic from Knaresborough or Harrogate, nor any place for the reception of parcels and merchandise. At Boroughbridge the agent of the York Newcastle & Berwick Railway, which now owned the main line between those places, as well as a branch from that railway to Boroughbridge, excelled at gaining business for that company. An omnibus service had been started solely to take Ripon people to Boroughbridge, where they could catch a train to Leeds, via York, and pay less than if they went direct from Ripon to Leeds by the L & T. The directors promised to look into these matters but looked mainly to the opening of their Stockton extension to solve their financial problems. This extension was formally opened on 15th May 1852 but not to passengers until 2nd June. Lack of money had led to the Melmerby - Picton section being laid as a single line.

The L & T changed its name to the Leeds Northern Railway in August 1851 but its finances improved little after the opening of the Stockton extension because of fierce competition from the YNMR and the York Newcastle & Berwick Railway (YN & B). Eventually the three companies agreed to work together and this led to amalgamation in July 1854. The new company was named the North Eastern Railway but the line from Leeds to Stockton via Starbeck and Ripon continued to be known as the Leeds Northern.

Three LNR stations underwent a change of name. Until November 1851 Melmerby station was called Wath, Arthington was Pool until February 1852, and until 1st June 1862 Nidd Bridge was called Ripley. In LNR days the station masters at both Melmerby and Nidd Bridge had been dismissed, the former for being "deficient in accounts", the latter for being drunk.

Although Harrogate was now well served by railways Harrogatonians considered none satisfactory. To catch a direct train to York, Leeds or the North meant travelling to Starbeck station, almost a mile from Harrogate. Omnibuses ran to the station but were said to be poor and inefficient with uncivil conductors who often overcharged. Brunswick station was in the town centre but trains took, on average, 50 minutes to run the 18½ miles to Church Fenton where there was often a long wait for a connection. After numerous requests to build a line from Starbeck to Harrogate the NER not only agreed to build such a line but also proposed to continue it to join the Church Fenton line near the south end of Brunswick Tunnel. Two other new lines, one from Bilton Jct. to Dragon Jct. and one from Crimple Jct. to Pannal Jct. would link the L & T to the Church Fenton line and enable trains between Leeds and the North to run through central Harrogate, where a new station was to be built. Knaresborough people opposed the scheme because they would have to pay higher fares and travel further to catch a main line train. To overcome this opposition the NER promised to allow fares from Knaresborough to any other station to be calculated according to the distance via the old line rather than the new. Some Harrogatonians also objected, because the line would cut through the Stray but this opposition was overcome after the NER agreed to give the site of Brunswick station, which was to be abandoned, as recompense for that part of the Stray taken. The NER also agreed to build an embankment 15 feet high to hide trains from one opponent who complained the sight of them would spoil the view from his house, Oatlands.

The Act authorising the new lines was obtained on 8th August 1859 but work did not begin until October 1860. In January 1861 severe weather brought work to a standstill. The workmen were laid off and might have starved had not Harrogatonians raised over £146 to buy them food and coal. The town authorities also helped by providing work clearing roads and footpaths of snow. By April 1862 work was progressing night and day. The works included the Bower Road Bridge, north of the new station. Although in a field it was thought the land might later be developed. The bridge consequently consisted of three arches, a central one for road vehicles and one at each side for pedestrians. The bridge collapsed when nearly completed and caused the opening of the new lines, and station, to be delayed until 1st August 1862. No one was hurt but elsewhere on the line two workmen died in separate accidents. It was during the construction of these new lines that the landlord of the Alexandra Hotel in West Park, Harrogate gained the nickname "Fiddle up Jerry". His wife would sit in the window and when she saw a navvy on his way from the works she would shout "Fiddle up Jerry" at which Jerry would dash into the street paying a lively tune on his fiddle in an attempt to lure the navvy into the bar.

In 1870 the station master at Pannal spent six months in prison for embezzlement, a crime the head goods clerk at Starbeck, and the chief booking clerk at Harrogate, were also found guilty of in 1868 and 1883 respectively.

In June 1880 a telegram was received at Leeds asking for the assistance of the Leeds fire brigade in fighting a fire at Nidd Hall. A fire engine and 12 men were immediately despatched to Leeds railway station but found the ordinary train had gone. A special train was therefore supplied. This ran non-stop from Leeds to Nidd Bridge in 45 minutes but on arrival found the Harrogate fire brigade had almost extinguished the blaze. After giving what assistance was required the Leeds men returned home by road at a more leisurely pace.

Prior to 1901 most trains between Harrogate and the North used the Melmerby – Thirsk line but in that year the Melmerby - Northallerton line was doubled and began to increase in importance.

During the First World War a line, which existed until the mid 1920s, was laid from the LNR line near Litttethorpe to an army camp near Ripon.

Signalling improvements in 1925 led to the closure of Brunswick signal box, just to the south of the Stray. Despite its name it had no connection with the old Brunswick station. Two years later Pannal Jct. box closed and thereafter the junction was worked from Pannal station box.

Between October 1934 and May 1935 the railway bridge at South Stainley was rebuilt to allow the road underneath to be widened. Complete occupation of the line meant that on some Sundays trains between Harrogate and the North were diverted over the Boroughbridge branch. The railway bridge over the Swale near Baldersby was also rebuilt, between May and August 1935.

During the Second World War a rail served Royal Ordnance Factory Store depot was opened at Melmerby. New signal boxes were opened here and at Monkton Moor, south of Ripon, where a loop on the up side capable of holding 76 wagons was opened on 22 September 1942. Increased traffic also led to the signal box at Bilton being extended where up and down goods loops were provided.

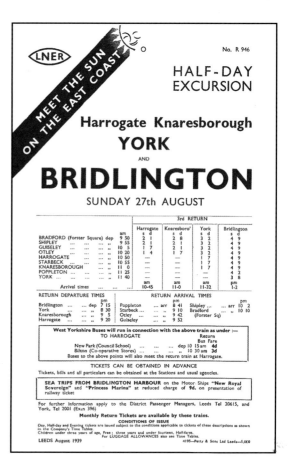

22

The poor condition of the Crimple Viaduct on the Pannal - Starbeck line led to the line's complete closure in 1951. Although regular passenger trains had not used the line since 12th September 1931, and few goods trains did so, its closure was strongly opposed by Harrogate Town Council who protested to Parliament, the British Transport Commission and the Army. The grave consequences that would follow the closure in the event of another war, or national emergency, were emphasised and it was pointed out that if anything happened to the other Crimple Viaduct, Harrogate, with the exception of the roundabout route via York, would be isolated from the South. The line closed on 26th May 1951, although the official closure date was not until 7th October 1951. Shortly after closure part of the trackbed was converted into a private road. The bridge by which the Harrogate - Wetherby road crossed the line was in poor condition by 1951. After the line's closure it was supported by buttresses until 1963 when it was demolished and the road made level. In NER days a signal box, Follifoot, had existed on the line, near the larger Crimple Viaduct. Another had controlled points leading to Stonefall Brickworks and a ground frame had controlled access to a siding serving Crimple Bleach Works.

The Melmerby - Thirsk line closed completely from 14th September 1959. However the former L & T terminus at Thirsk, which had closed to passengers as long ago as 1856, remained open for goods until 1966. The line had declined in importance after the doubling of the Melmerby - Northallerton line in 1901 and in later years had been worked as a single line, the other line being used to store wagons.

Many goods trains between Teesside and the West Riding used the Leeds Northern so as not to hinder passenger trains using the East Coast Main line between Northallerton and York. In 1954 the average number of wagons on each goods train using the Leeds Northern was 35 but by 1959 the number had fallen to 25. A further blow was the decision to complete the quadrupling of the ECML between Northallerton and York and transfer to it the goods trains using the Leeds Northern. Although this quadrupling was not completed until 9th June 1960 goods trains were transferred away from the Leeds Northern on 13th September 1959. By 1963 the only through goods trains using the line were the Newport - Heysham Moss tanker trains which ran via Otley.

By July 1962 the only stations still open to passengers between Harrogate and Northallerton were Ripon and Melmerby. Newby Wiske had closed as long ago as 11th September 1939, Pickhill had closed on 14th September 1959 and Sinderby on 1st January 1962. Wormald Green and Nidd Bridge had both lost their passenger service from 18th June 1962. There had been opposition to the closure of Nidd Bridge, because there was no alternate bus service, but BR had claimed the station's main users were 25 shoppers who went to Harrogate on Saturdays. In 1963 Beeching announced the withdrawal of passenger services between Harrogate, Ripon and Northallerton. Withdrawal was to have taken place from 30th November 1964 but this was postponed after 173 objections were received and consent to close the line was not given until 20 September 1966. The Harrogate - York line had also been proposed for closure but consent for this was refused. With the York line saved Harrogate Council's opposition to the closure of the

NIDD BRIDGE
c.1930 - 38

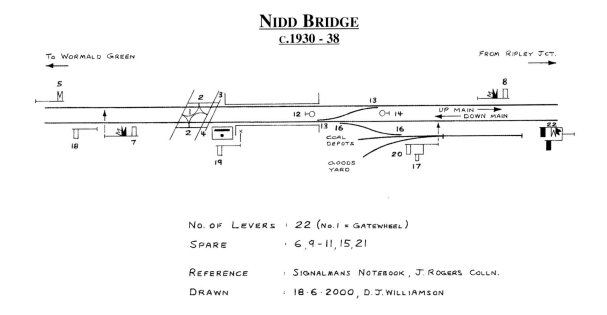

NO. OF LEVERS : 22 (No.1 = GATEWHEEL)

SPARE : 6,9-11,15,21

REFERENCE : SIGNALMANS NOTEBOOK, J. ROGERS COLLN.

DRAWN : 18·6·2000, D.J. WILLIAMSON

Plate 2.6   The station building at Wormald Green was the second on this site, this structure being erected in 1865. A small goods yard was provided for local trade beyond the crossing with one siding further back serving a limestone quarry. The signal box seen in the background to the left of the level crossing was replaced in the 1920's.   Ken Hoole collection.

Plate 2.7   LMS Jubilee class No. 45562, 'Alberta' heads the empty stock of the Royal Train 'wrong line' through Wormald Green on 30th May 1967 – only one track was used for freight services as far as Melmerby after the closure to passengers. The Royal Train had earlier conveyed Prince Philip from York to Nidd Bridge. To run round its train it had to run through to Ripon before returning to York.   D.J. Williamson collection.

Northallerton line was diminished but Ripon City Council continued to fight, even after 6th March 1967 when the passenger service between Harrogate and Northallerton, via Ripon, was withdrawn. They proposed the line be reopened as a single line with unmanned stations but BR considered this would not make the line profitable.

On 30th May 1967, shortly after the withdrawal of passenger traffic, Prince Philip alighted at Nidd Bridge to visit the Army Apprentice College. The Royal Train was hauled from York to Nidd Bridge, via Starbeck, by 'Jubilee' Class 4-6-0, No. 45562 "Alberta", which later returned the train to York as empty stock having run round the train at Ripon.

Whenever the main line between York and Northallerton had been blocked trains had been diverted via Starbeck and Ripon. An accident near Thirsk involving prototype Diesel DP2 caused down trains to be so diverted from 31st July to 2nd August 1967 over the Melmerby - Northallerton section. This section, which had been closed completely, had to be temporarily reopened. By 1965, north of Harrogate, only Ripon and the ordnance supply depot at Melmerby remained open for goods. This traffic however did not long survive the withdrawal of the passenger service and the last goods train, hauled by Class 20 loco No. 8301, ran on 9th October 1969.

South of Harrogate the only closed passenger station is Arthington, passenger services being withdrawn from 22nd March 1965. On a brighter note two new stations have been opened, Burley Park on 28th November 1988 and Hornbeam Park, Oatlands, on 24th August 1992. Ironically, exactly 100 years earlier, in 1892, the NER had turned down a request for a station at Oatlands. By June 1965 all stations south of Harrogate had lost their goods traffic. The closure of the goods yards led to the elimination of most of the signal boxes on the line, only Rigton and Horsforth surviving. Single line working was resorted to between Rigton and Horsforth for approximately six weeks in March/April 1977 after part of the embankment near the Wharfe Viaduct subsided. Trains had been worked on a single line between Arthington and Horsforth for about six months in 1934/5 while Bramhope Tunnel was repaired. From 30th June 1980 to 1st June 1981 repairs to the tunnel again made single line working between those places necessary but the signal boxes at Arthington had long been demolished and a temporary box, and temporary signals, had to be provided.

All intermediate stations on the Leeds - Harrogate - York line, with the exception of Harrogate, became unstaffed halts from 15th June 1969 when conductor guards were introduced on all local trains. At Pannal the station house was converted into a public house. This opened in 1980 as "Platform One". The following year a Pullman car was acquired to act as a restaurant. Originally Parlour Kitchen car No. 332 it was renamed "Mae" on arrival at Pannal. More recently the public house has changed hands with a name change to the "The Harwood" whilst the Pullman car was cut up by a Rotherham scrap merchant.

Weeton station was rebuilt in 1865. One night in June 1910 thieves broke into it, blew open the safe and stole its contents of about £5. The stationmaster, who lived close by, and the signalman at Rigton, both heard the explosion, which also smashed several of the station's windows, but mistook it for thunder. The previous robbery at the station had occurred only five weeks earlier. On 13th July 1995 a fire, thought to have been started by children playing underneath, destroyed the down side station building.

WORMALD GREEN

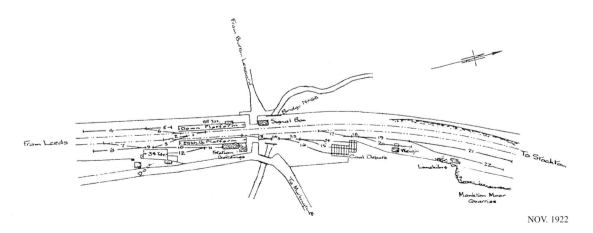

NOV. 1922

25

Plate 2.8   The Queen of Scots hauled by LNER Gresley class A3, No. 60084, 'Trigo', passes the wartime up loop and signal box at Monkton Moor. J.W.Hague/J. Rogers collection.

Plate 2.9   Melmerby station, sited at the divergence of the Thirsk, Northallerton and Masham lines, was just to the north of the level crossing. This view of the crossing and South signal box was taken prior to the rearrangement of the station platforms and track layout in 1913. The result of this was the rebuilding of the box and the closing of Melmerby North signal box, which had controlled the earlier junction with the Masham branch. Ken Hoole collection.

Chapter 3

PASSENGER SERVICES ON THE LEEDS NORTHERN

On weekdays in March 1850 trains left Starbeck for the north at 9 04 am, 11.43 am, 2 04 pm, 5.04 pm and 7.43 pm and on Sundays at 8.49 am and 7.19 pm. Southbound departures, on weekdays, were at 9.26 am, 11.30 am, 2.33 pm, 6.05 pm, 7.08 pm and on Sundays at 9.00 am and 7.28 pm.

With the opening of the Leeds Northern's Stockton extension in June 1852 came a new timetable. Passenger trains left Starbeck, on weekdays, for the North at 6.15 am, 8.45 am, 11.40 am, 4.54 pm, 5.15 pm, and 7.40 pm and for the South at 8.00 am, 9.20 am, 11.50 am, 2.16 pm, 3.15 pm, 6.08 pm, and 7.15 pm. In addition there were goods trains to the North at 5.00 am, 7.20 am, 12.30 pm, and 9.10 pm and to the South at 6.00 am, 7.35 am, 5.00 pm, and 7.10 pm.

Harrogatonians welcomed the coming of the railways. In 1848 the Editor of the "Harrogate Advertiser" wished some genius would invent steam wings so more people might visit the town. In 1852 however the Editor was among prominent Harrogatonians who persuaded the LNR not to run some Sunday excursions which they believed would desecrate the Sabbath. In 1904 some town councillors opposed Sunday excursion trains to Harrogate because they did not want the town to become a pandemonium on Sundays, like Scarborough. Others welcomed excursion trains because if trippers could not come by train they would come by wagonettes which stopped at every public house on the way.

In NER days there were frequent complaints about unpunctual trains and missed connections. In 1871 a Wetherby passenger, after once again missing his connection at Harrogate, took a cab to his destination and later took the NER to court in an unsuccessful attempt to recover his cab fare. Some felt the fear of travelling through Bramhope Tunnel, and round the Crimple curve, dissuaded people from coming to Harrogate. One man stated he would sooner cross the Bay of Biscay in a storm then travel through Bramhope Tunnel and over Crimple Viaduct, while another described the Leeds - Harrogate line as "about as nasty a bit of railway as could be found in the entire kingdom." Others felt the NER abused its monopoly and that another company should be encouraged to build a line into the town. In 1877 the town authorities asked the Midland Railway, unsuccessfully, to build a line, or take up running powers, into Harrogate. The following year they asked the Great Eastern Railway, also without success, to extend their proposed Long Stanton - Askern line to Harrogate.

Passenger services on the Leeds Northern increased over the years. From 1883 the London & North Western Railway provided a through Liverpool - Newcastle service, via Harrogate. This meant NER locos could be seen hauling LNWR carriages through the town. In 1907 there were three trains in each direction per weekday, two of which ran via Wetherby. In 1897 the Lancashire & Yorkshire Railway began a through service between Liverpool and Harrogate, which after 1901 was worked throughout by L & Y locos. In summer 1904 there were three trains in each direction on weekdays but the last from Harrogate, at 8.12 pm, terminated at Manchester.

The railway enabled many people to live in Harrogate and work in Leeds. In 1885 Horsforth commuters, or passholders as they were then called, asked the NER to stop the 2.15 pm Harrogate - Leeds and the 5.30 pm Leeds - Harrogate expresses at Horsforth. Harrogate passholders successfully counter petitioned the NER, arguing the 2.15 pm made connections at Holbeck which might be lost if it was interfered with, and the 5.30 pm was always overcrowded and often ran late. One passholder said he had not known it arrive on time since 1871. If it was made available to Horsforth passengers it would be more overcrowded and even less punctual. The needs of Horsforth passholders could be met by stopping some Leeds - Ilkley via Arthington, trains at Horsforth. A passholder in 1893 estimated there were between 1,000 and 1,200 passholders between Harrogate and Leeds but the NER showed them about as much consideration as cheap excursionists. The 8.35 am Harrogate – Leeds often started late and connections were missed. Once the train arrived at Harrogate short of carriages and about 100 passengers could not find seats. The addition of extra carriages caused 15 minutes delay and three more were lost on the journey. Trains were also delayed while horse boxes were attached, or detached, and he believed the NER ought to show its regular customers more consideration, but no, one horse box to attach, or detach, was, apparently, of more importance than the convenience of about 500 or more, businessmen.

Plate 3.1   A NER Raven design class Z 'Atlantic', No.2210, passing south through Harrogate's Stray with up 11.15 am Pullman working sometime before 1928. 12-wheel Pullmans (class K), built by the Clayton Wagon Co., were used in the period 1923-8. They also exhibit the Pullman livery prior to 1929 in which year the panels just below the roof line of the cars was changed from cream to umber brown as coaches were due for works attention. At this time permanent way staff were allowed to cultivate the embankments as allotments.   D.J. Williamson collection.

Plate 3.2   A rare view of the almost new LNER class A4 'Pacific' No.2511 'Silver King' at Ripon with the afternoon 2.15pm Liverpool – Newcastle service in the summer of 1936. Whilst the main part of the train is comprised of LNWR/LMS stock, the first three vehicles would have been added at Leeds. These are two LNER Gresley design coaches and an ex-NER Open Third converted to a Buffet Car. This loco was one of the first four of its class; the others were No.2509 'Silver Link', No.2510 'Quicksilver', and No.2512 'Silver Fox'.   G. Pierson collection.

Despite the improvements made to the station in the late 1890s some complained the platforms and carriages were filthy and antiquated footwarmers the only heating provided in the latter. One person wished the Midland Railway would extend to Harrogate because goods from the Midlands took a week to arrive and often arrived damaged. In many towns when a tradesman wanted a railway dray to call he hung a card in his window but in Harrogate if a dray was required he had to write asking for one to call. The excessive speed of trains over the Crimple curve was also complained of. One man wrote in 1900, "Tonight the 8 o' clock train from Leeds was 15 minutes late at Holbeck but by travelling at an excessive speed actually reduced its lateness to seven minutes at Harrogate. It might be quite safe to travel round so sharp a curve at 40 mph but the uninitiated cannot bring themselves to think so and the manifest terror of eight passengers in the compartment in which I travelled, and the extreme discomfort occasioned by the violent oscillations, were sufficient to convince me a protest was needful. This speed is only maintained when the train happens to be late and the driver reckless. We are continually suffering from the inability of this monopolistic railway company to keep time, need we have our safety jeopardised by this sort of thing?"

In 1901 complaints were made about the price of season tickets. In 1900 a first class ticket from Harrogate to Leeds had cost £15 a year, while a third class ticket had cost £9. In 1901, because of the increased price of coal, the price of a first class ticket had been increased to £18, and a third class to £10. Despite a fall in the price of coal it was announced that in 1902 an annual first class ticket would cost £21 10s 0d, and a third class £11 15s 0d. Over 200 passholders, and the Harrogate Traders Association, protested and as a result the increases were not fully implemented. From 1st January 1902 the price of an annual first class ticket became £19 15s 0d, and the price of a third £10 12s 6d.

In 1905 Harrogate Traders Association asked for additional trains between Leeds and Harrogate around noon to enable businessmen to return home for dinner. This request was refused because the NER believed businessmen would find four journeys a day too much. After running a test train on 11th May 1902 the Great Northern Railway began, from 1st July 1902, a service of through trains between Kings Cross and Harrogate, via Doncaster, Knottingley, Church Fenton and Spofforth. These ran as follows: -

	AM	PM	PM
Kings Cross dep.	11.25	1.40	3.45
Harrogate arr.	3.28	5.42	7.57

The 11.25 am continued to Edinburgh where it arrived at 7.55 pm.

	AM	PM	PM
Harrogate dep.	9.55	2.28	4.44
Kings Cross arr.	2.10	6.50	8.45

The 4.44 pm started from Edinburgh at 12.30 pm.

Prior to 1902 there had been through carriages between Kings Cross and Harrogate, via York, a service known unofficially as the "Majestic". Some GNR trains were soon extended to Ripon and proved so popular that in 1907 the GNR had to reassure the Dean of Ripon there was no truth in a rumour they were to be withdrawn.

The Midland Railway also began a through service between London and Harrogate from 1st July 1902 with trains running as follows: -

	AM	PM	PM
St Pancras dep.	9.30	12.15	5.00
Harrogate arr.	2.12	5.57	10.00

	AM	AM	PM
Harrogate dep.	10.15	3.00	6.22
St Pancras arr.	3.40	7.50	11.05

Plate 3.3 A BR Derby Lightweight DMU takes the Leeds line at Arthington North Junction whilst on a Harrogate – Bradford Exchange working via Leeds Central. These DMUs were the first to be introduced on a fleet basis in 1954, this early design having a larger glass panelled front end compared to later designs. To the left of the train Arthington's goods accommodation provided a loading dock and coal cells. Behind this the Wharfe Valley stretches out towards Armscliffe Crag.   Ken Hoole collection.

Plate 3.4   The 11.0 am 'Queen of Scots' Glasgow to London Kings Cross service (1E14) headed by English Electric Type 4, No. 348, has just passed the station and signal box at Melmerby. The Pullmans are a mix of the then new Metro-Cammell cars built in 1960/61 and the older straight sided brake seconds dating from 1928.   Ken Hoole collection..

The following summer the Midland also introduced a through carriage between Bournemouth and Harrogate.

By 1902 both the GNR and the Midland had opened offices in Harrogate, the GNR at 3 Station Bridge and the Midland at 8 Crescent Road. The GNR later moved to 16 James Street. Locos of both companies, including GNR Atlantics, were stationed at Starbeck shed.

Through trains between Harrogate and St Pancras ceased during the First World War and soon after the Midland Railway closed its Harrogate office. In April 1922 Harrogate Corporation, on behalf of the Harrogate branch of the Commercial Travellers Association, requested the trains be reinstated and were informed that from 1st May they would be. The Midland also reopened its Harrogate Office in new premises at 20 Crescent Road. Through trains between Harrogate and St. Pancras continued to be provided by the LMS. In summer 1925 trains ran as follows: -

	PM	PM
St Pancras dep.	12.05	5.00
Harrogate arr.	4.50	10.13

	PM	PM
Harrogate dep.	12.03	6.05
St Pancras arr.	4.55	10.55

Some of these trains ran via the Pannal - Starbeck line in one direction to avoid reversal at Harrogate. The service was withdrawn in 1928 and around 1935 the LMS closed its Harrogate office. The GNR office was retained by the LNER.

In 1923 the LNER agreed to a request from Harrogate Corporation and provided the town with an all Pullman Car train, the "Harrogate Pullman". A special run was made from Kings Cross to Harrogate on 30th June 1923 when Harrogate Corporation provided 150 guests of the LNER and Pullman Car Company with refreshments at the Hotel Majestic. Amongst the guests were Oliver Bulleid, the LNER's Assistant Chief Mechanical Engineer, and Ralph Wedgwood, the LNER's General Manager. Wedgwood, who had lived at Stonefall Hall, Starbeck, ten years earlier, was knighted in 1939. One of the LNER's Class A4 Pacifics was also named after him. The Pullman train returned to London following day after public inspection at Harrogate station.

The "Harrogate Pullman" commenced running on 9th July 1923. The down train left Kings Cross at 11.25 am, Harrogate at 3.20 pm and arrived in Newcastle at 5.00 pm, having also called at Leeds, Ripon and Darlington. The up train left Newcastle at 9.20 am, Harrogate at 11.15 am and arrived in London at 3.15 pm, having called at the same stations as the down train. Between Leeds and Newcastle it was usually hauled by an ex NER Atlantic.

In July 1925 Edinburgh became the northern terminus. The times of the down train remained unchanged and Edinburgh was reached at 7.50 pm. The up train left Edinburgh at 8.30 am, Harrogate at 1.05 pm, and reached Kings Cross at 5.05 pm. From September 1925 another Pullman train was introduced. This left Kings Cross at 11.10 am for Leeds, but in the opposite direction it started from Harrogate at 11.15 am and, after calling at Leeds, arrived in London at 3.15 pm. This meant Harrogate now had two Pullmans to London but only one from London. Because the new 11.10 am from Kings Cross would serve Leeds it was decided from 21st September 1925 that the "Harrogate Pullman" would no longer travel via Leeds but would run non-stop between Kings Cross and Harrogate, via Shaftholme Jct., Knottingley, Church Fenton and Spofforth. This was a distance of 198.8 miles, 5 miles less than the route via Leeds. Departure from Kings Cross was altered to 11.20 am with arrival in Harrogate at 3.03 pm and Edinburgh at 7.35 pm. In the opposite direction Edinburgh was departed at 8.30 am, Harrogate at 1.05 pm and Kings Cross reached at 4.45 pm. Although locos were changed at Harrogate, Starbeck locos played no part, except sometimes to assist the train the last few miles into Harrogate after its loco had run out of coal on the non stop run. Locos for the Kings Cross - Harrogate section were provided by Kings Cross and Copley Hill, Leeds, sheds. At first Class B3 4-6-0's, were provided but by 1927 Class D11 4-4-0s, and Class C1 4-4-2s had taken over. The loco which was to work the train south reached Harrogate by bringing in the empty Pullman cars that were to form the 11.15 am Harrogate - Kings Cross. The loco working the down "Harrogate Pullman" would, after arrival in Harrogate, reach Leeds by taking out an ordinary Harrogate - Leeds passenger train. Ex NER Atlantics continued to work the train north of Harrogate but Gresley Pacifics later took over. After bringing the up train into Harrogate the loco would retire to Starbeck shed before returning north with the down train.

Following discussions between Harrogate Chamber of Trade and the LNER the "Harrogate Sunday Pullman" was introduced on 17th July 1927. This left Kings Cross at 10.30 am and arrived in Leeds at 1.55 pm. After detaching cars for Bradford, Harrogate was reached at 2.30 pm. On the return journey the train left Harrogate at 3.15 pm, Leeds at 3.50 pm and arrived at Kings Cross at 7.15 pm. A large crowd watched the departure of the first train from Harrogate, with 66 passengers.

After extension to Edinburgh the "Harrogate Pullman" became known as the "Edinburgh Pullman" but in 1927 it was renamed the "Queen of Scots". From 1st May 1928 the train was re-routed to serve Leeds again and extended to Glasgow. It now left Kings Cross at 11.15 am, Harrogate at 3.20 pm and arrived in Glasgow Queen Street at 8.45 pm. In the opposite direction it left Glasgow at 10.05 am and arrived in Harrogate at 3.31 pm and Kings Cross at 7.35 pm. Alterations were also made to the 11.10 am Kings Cross - Leeds and the 11.15 am Harrogate –Kings Cross Pullmans. This service was extended to serve Harrogate in both directions but now also served Ripon, Darlington and Newcastle. Now named the "West Riding Pullman" this train left Newcastle at 9.10 am, Harrogate at 11.00 am and after calling at Leeds and Wakefield arrived at Kings Cross at 3.00 pm. On the return journey departure from Kings Cross was at 4.45 pm with arrival in Harrogate at 8.50 pm and Newcastle at 10.27 pm.

In September 1935 the "Silver Jubilee" was introduced between Kings Cross and Newcastle, via York. So as not to compete the "West Riding Pullman" was reduced to a Kings Cross – Harrogate service and renamed the "Yorkshire Pullman". Two years later in September 1937, it was re-routed, in the up direction only, via York instead of Leeds, so as not to duplicate the "West Riding Limited" introduced between Kings Cross and Leeds that month.

In 1939 the "Yorkshire Pullman" left Harrogate at 11.15 am, York at 11.45 am and arrived in London at 3.00 pm. The down train left Kings Cross at 4.45 pm, Leeds at 8.17 pm and arrived in Harrogate at 8.45 pm.

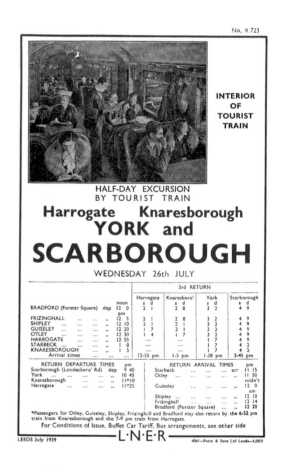

32

At this time there were also three ordinary through trains in each direction each weekday between Harrogate and Kings Cross. These ran as follows; -

	AM	PM	PM
Harrogate dep.	9.32	12.20	4.45
Kings Cross arr.	1.47	4.50	9.25

The 9.32 am started from Ripon at 9.05 am. On Saturdays the 12.20 pm left at 11.55 am and arrived in Kings Cross at 4.33 pm.

	AM	PM	PM
Kings Cross dep.	10.15	1.40	5.50
Harrogate arr.	2.45	6.10	10.17

All ran via Leeds except the 1.40 pm from Kings Cross which ran via Church Fenton.

The Pullmans were withdrawn on the outbreak of war in 1939. After the war the "Yorkshire Pullman", running via Leeds in both directions, was reintroduced on 11th November 1946. It was withdrawn in March 1947 because of a coal shortage but reinstated on 6 October 1947.

The "Queen of Scots" was reintroduced on 5th July 1948. Neville Hill shed, Leeds, later became responsible for working the train in both directions between Leeds and Newcastle and usually provided two locos from its stud of five Class A3 Pacifics, Nos. 60036 "Colombo", 60074 "Harvester", 60081 "Shotover", 60084 "Trigo" and 60086 "Gainsborough. If these were not available a York loco would be borrowed. In the early 1960s Class 40 and later Deltic diesel locos took over the working but by 1964 the number of passengers north of Harrogate did not justify the train's existence and it ran no more after 13th June 1964. It was replaced between Kings Cross and Leeds by a new Pullman train, the 'White Rose" which from 7th September 1964 included a Harrogate portion. At withdrawal the "Queen of Scots" had left Kings Cross at 12 noon and arrived in Harrogate at 3.52 pm. The up train had left Harrogate at 3.46 pm and arrived at Kings Cross at 7.45 pm. The 'White Rose" left Kings Cross at 11.40 am and arrived in Harrogate at 3.23 pm while the up train left Harrogate at 4.00 pm and arrived at Kings Cross at 7.40 pm. Both the 'White Rose" and the "Harrogate Sunday Pullman", which had been rein-troduced on 11 June 1950, ceased to run after March 1967. The "Yorkshire Pullman ceased to be an all Pullman car train in 1971 and was withdrawn on 5th May 1978 to allow the introduction of High Speed Trains (HST).

In summer 1950 there were two non-Pullman trains in both directions between Harrogate and Kings Cross, one of which also served Ripon in both directions. On Sundays there was one non Pullman train in each direction between Harrogate and Kings Cross. In Summer 1966, as well as the Pullmans, there was, Mondays to Fridays, one train from Harrogate to Kings Cross but no through train in the opposite direction. On Saturdays and Sundays there was one train in each direction. Summer 1979 saw three trains in each direction between Harrogate and Kings Cross on weekdays and one in each direction on Sundays. By summer 1984 there was only one train each day, including Sundays, from Harrogate to Kings Cross but in the opposite direction there were two, Mondays to Fridays, and one on Saturdays and Sundays. In 1989 trains, hauled by electric Class 91 locos, began working the evening Kings Cross - Harrogate train. This train was hauled from Leeds by a Class 47 diesel loco and after calling at Harrogate continued to York as empty stock. A trial run from Leeds to Harrogate and back had been made on 3rd April 1989 using a Class 47 diesel loco to haul 91 008 with stock and a HST Driving Van Trailer coach. Later the electric loco was detached at Leeds and only the coaches were hauled to Harrogate. From 11th May 1992 the train ceased to run. The morning Harrogate - Kings Cross continued, in the shape of a HST, but there was no through return service from Kings Cross.

In the 1930s a diesel electric- railcar "Northumbrian", based at Leeds, had worked in the Harrogate area and 1944 a Great Western Railway diesel railcar. No 19, worked from Starbeck shed on trials, In August 1952 another, W20W, ran trials between Harrogate and Leeds. Two years later the Bradford Exchange - Leeds Central - Harrogate service became the first in Britain on which BR diesel multiple units were used. A press run was made on 8th June 1954 and the service proper began six days later, with some trains running through to Knaresborough on Sundays. Despite breakdowns the number of passengers using the Harrogate - Leeds line increased by more than 28,000 by the end of the year and on some public holidays in the 1950s diesel trains from the West Riding to Knaresborough had to be supplemented by steam trains.

Plate 3.5   LNER class D49 4-4-0 No.62736 'The Bramham Moor' makes an impressive start along Harrogate's Stray on the 14.20 Harrogate –
Kings Cross train on the 29th April 1956. The first three vehicles are LNER Thompson design coaches. J. Edgington.

Plate 3.6   A Kirtley designed Midland Railway 2-4-0, No. 156A stands on the Harrogate turntable – The Midland introduced a through service from
London St. Pancras via Leeds Wellington Street in July 1902. Built in September 1866 this engine was renumbered No. 1 in 1907 but was not with-
drawn from use until 1930.   G. Pierson collection.

On 19th September 1955 the first regular diesel service to Ripon began. After 5th January 1959 the only steam hauled local stopping trains were the 3.57 am Leeds - Ripon and the trains from Harrogate to Leeds, via Wetherby, at 7.30 am, 12.30 pm Saturdays only, 4.40 pm Saturdays excepted and 6.00 pm Saturdays only. In the opposite direction the 4.19 pm Saturdays only and the 5.35 pm Saturdays excepted were steam hauled.

On 1st January 1962 a through DMU service was introduced between Harrogate and Liverpool Exchange, via Leeds Central, Bradford Exchange and Manchester Victoria. In summer that year there were, Mondays to Fridays, ten trains to Manchester, four of which continued to Liverpool. On Saturdays one normally terminating at Manchester continued to Southport. In the opposite direction there were, Mondays to Fridays, ten trains, three of which started from Liverpool, six from Manchester and one from Sowerby Bridge. On Saturdays one train started from Southport, not Manchester. On Sundays passengers in both directions had to change at Bradford. By 1967, when the service was withdrawn, a stop had been included at Wigan Wallgate.

As well as the above, over the years, the Leeds Northern was used by a variety of expresses, including some between Sheffield Midland and Craigendoran, and Llandudno and Newcastle, but the majority of passenger trains had been local stopping trains. When the Harrogate - Northallerton line closed to passengers there were ten down and nine up passenger trains using the line each weekday, and five down and three up on Sundays. These included two in each direction between Liverpool and Newcastle on weekdays, and one in each direction between Manchester and Newcastle on Sundays. All stopped at Ripon. North of Northallerton some trains ran via Sunderland rather than Darlington. Today, with the exception of one train to London, Harrogate only sees local stopping trains. From May 1984 Class 141, 142 and 144 "Pacer" railbuses were introduced on local trains and the timetable improved. Between 6 00 and 20 00 hours an almost half-hourly service was provided between Leeds and Harrogate on weekdays instead of the previously almost hourly service. Most of these trains have also been extended to Knaresborough. Also York has been provided with an almost hourly service from Harrogate. All local trains became second class only with the abolition of first class from 24th January 1983 and all became non-smoking from 1st November 1991. Privatisation saw the Great North Eastern Railway take over the running of the Harrogate - Kings Cross train from 28th April 1996 and MTL took over the operation of all local services from Harrogate on 2nd March 1997 (who re-branded their rail operations as 'Northern Spirit'). With the withdrawal of the earliest railbuses - the Class 141s, "Sprinters" of Classes 150, 153 and 156 have been introduced on the York – Harrogate – Leeds services.

Plate 3.7 A rare view of NER class R 4-4-0, No. 2024 climbing the last few yards into Harrogate with a Newcastle - Liverpool express train formed of London & North Western Railway arc-roof stock - an NER coach has been added at the front to provide extra seating. Harrogate enjoyed three such through trains daily around the time of this view, c1905-10. The north end of Harrogate was remodelled and resignalled in 1898, Harrogate North signal box just being visible to the left of the engine. A 50'0" diameter engine turntable was provided at the same time being located to the right of the approaching train. Note the old six wheel coaches and open carriage truck stabled on the left. G. Pierson collection.

Plate 4.1   Station Bridge seen before the rebuilding works in the late 1890's when the approach road to the up side platform was excavated to form to two bay platforms. Two houses in East Parade were demolished to make a new approach road. Whilst the ornate cast iron parapets are no longer to be seen on Station Bridge they are still to be seen on Westminster Bridge (Victoria Avenue) and Royal Bridge (York Place).   Ken Hoole Collection.

Plate 4.2   The old, not so old and new. Ex-NER class D20, No.62387 (built April 1907) and an unidentified LNER class A1 (introduced 1948-9) double heading a southbound Newcastle – Liverpool train past a BR Derby Lightweight DMU between Station Bridge and Westminster Bridge. The class D20 was withdrawn in September 1957 from Alnmouth shed.   Ken Hoole collection

Chapter 4

HARROGATE STATION

There was no official ceremony to mark the opening of Harrogate station on 1st August 1862 but a large crowd cheered in the first train, the 5.52 am arrival from Leeds. At first the station had only one platform and to avoid reversal some trains between Leeds and Harrogate ran via Starbeck in one direction. The first station master, Charles Matthews, had held similar positions at Pannal, Newby Wiske, Yarm, Arthington and Starbeck and before joining the railway had been a stage coach driver on the Leeds - Harrogate - Knaresborough route. In 1866 he spent six months in hospital after being attacked by militiamen he was trying to evict from the station.

Although a platform was opened on the east side of the station in 1866 it was not immediately asphalted and most trains continued to use the west platform. In 1872 a train was derailed north of the station. No one was hurt but the investigating officer reported that if Harrogate ceased to be worked as a one sided station some facing points could be eliminated and similar accidents would be less likely to occur. In 1873 a footbridge linking the two platforms was provided. Ten years later the station roof was extended. In the late 1890s the east side platform was extended at the south end under the station bridge. Here two bay platforms were created. This destroyed the roadway leading to the east side of the station but a new access road was made by demolishing two houses in East Parade. A signal box on the north west side of Station Bridge was replaced by a new box on the south west side. In addition the footbridge at the station's south end, was replaced by one in a central position. Two goods bays in the station yard, reached via a small turntable, remained unaltered. Despite these improvements the local press complained in 1902 the station was too small and the refreshment rooms inadequate to the demands made upon them. In 1914 the town council thought the station not only inadequate but a disgrace to both the town and the railway company.

In 1907 519,293 tickets were issued from Harrogate station, 21,078 of which were excursion tickets. The number of tickets collected at Harrogate in 1907 was 948,955, of these 64,514 were excursion tickets.

Improvements were made to the east side in 1924. A new entrance and a glass veranda, to protect passengers alighting from cars from the rain, were provided. The booking hall was enlarged and the steps of the footbridge made to lead straight ahead instead of branching off to the sides. Ticket barriers, which already existed on the west side, were now provided on the east. Immediately prior to this tickets from passengers arriving from the north had been collected at the previous stop. Between the wars the LNER and Harrogate Corporation were on very friendly terms. In 1928 the LNER sold some property, including the former stationmaster's house in Station Square, Harrogate, to Harrogate Corporation for £21,500, although they could have obtained a higher price from a commercial buyer.

In 1929 the station offices, waiting rooms and refreshment room were equipped with electric lighting in anticipation of crowds attending the Royal Agricultural Show, held in Harrogate that year. In the same year Harrogate station's down platform was resignalled to enable up trains to use it once more. The railings and advertising hoardings were removed from the front of the station in 1934 and flowerbeds laid out. The waiting rooms were also improved and on 13th May a new booking office opened on the west side.

Bell keys were provided for trains leaving the north end of the station. When pressed they operated an indicator in Harrogate North box which told the signalman the line the driver required. On some platforms, where a curve meant the driver could not see the guard at the rear, electric starting bells were provided to expedite departure. The guard would operate the appropriate bell and the driver could take it, instead of the green flag or lamp, as the signal to start. In 1938 Harrogate South signalbox received a new 45 lever frame and around 1946 Harrogate North box was replaced by the present North box on the opposite side of the line.

The west side of Harrogate station was completely rebuilt during 1963-5 to provide shops and an office block. At various times in the 1970s the station buildings and roof on the east side were demolished and the rubble used to fill the bays on the north east side. In January 1981 the remaining line in the bay on the south-east side was lifted which, with signalling alterations, resulted in the closure of Harrogate South box. In 1985 part of the cutting south of the station was roofed over to form a supermarket car park, and in 1993 the station footbridge was replaced by one further north in connection with a multi storey car park built on the site of the north east bays. From 1st April 1994 the station and the Leeds - Harrogate – York line became the property of Railtrack.

A HARROGATE MYSTERY

On the arrival of the 3.21 pm Leeds - Thirsk at Harrogate on 10 July 1900 a young man drew the attention of a porter to a parcel left in his compartment. The parcel, which bore only the words, "Smith, Darlington", was taken to the left luggage office where it was opened the following day and found to contain the body of a baby. At an inquest, two weeks later, it was stated that despite widespread inquires and appeals the passenger who had called the porter's attention to the parcel had not been traced. On a happier note a passenger gave birth to a son in the ladies first class waiting room in 1895.

STRIKES

During Britain's second national railway strike the first train into Harrogate arrived from Leeds at 4.10 pm on 30th September 1919, four days after the strike began. Its driver is said to have worn a trilby and looked a toff. The train left for Leeds 20 minutes later watched by a large crowd on Station Bridge.

When the General Strike began, on 4th May 1926, Harrogate station was closed. Taxi drivers with little to do played football in the station yard, but well filled buses ran. The Harrogate division of British Fascists was quick to respond to appeals for help in keeping trains running. Twelve fascists were immediately enrolled in the special railway police, and eight others sent to Starbeck to deal with perishable goods. At Harrogate 24 fascists, under 2 officers, were among volunteers who dealt with passengers, parcels and over 11,000 gallons of milk during the nine day strike. Volunteer porters could be seen in "plus fours" and when a loco damaged points volunteer platelayers soon had them repaired. When a train arrived from Leeds with windows

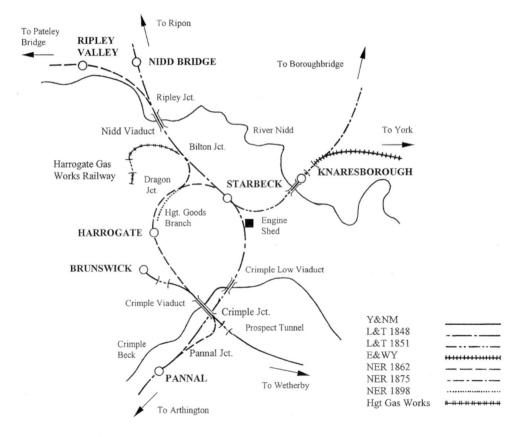

RAILWAYS OF HARROGATE

washed, handles polished, and a note saying this was how Leeds volunteers sent out trains the Harrogate men ensure the next train to Leeds was scrubbed, polished and sent as Harrogate's answer. On 6th May two trains in each direction were run between Harrogate and York, and between Leeds and Ripon. On 12th May a newspaper, published by the LNER, reported under the heading "Hurrah for Harrogate" that the strike was making little difference to the town, train services from London and other cities were good and no visitor was suffering the slightest inconvenience. The same issue, however, reported mail was being taken from Leeds to Harrogate by road and a motorist had found a mailbag that had fallen from a lorry at Harewood bridge.

MOTOR BUSES

Motor buses appeared in Harrogate before the First World War. In 1913 one visitor called these "wretched rattletrap cars" a disgrace to the town and thought it unlikely such "poverty stricken cars" could be found in any other town. One resident believed these "dilapidated and out of date vehicles" might do for a fourth rate small manufacturing town but were quite unsuitable for a high class residential and pleasure resort such as Harrogate, and he hoped the Corporation would insist on their replacement with smart up to date motor buses. In 1921, when complaints were made about overcrowding on Harrogate - Knaresborough trains, one complainant added, significantly, they would be more overcrowded if some former railway passengers did not now go by bus. By 1930 buses were running from Harrogate to many major cities and employees of the West Yorkshire Road Car Company were asking the Harrogate branch of the National Union of Railwaymen to instruct them in trade union practice. The same year the local press remarked that great changes had occurred at Harrogate's railway station in the previous ten years. Once passengers were hurried along but now there seemed hardly anyone to hurry along, buses, with their up to the minute arrangements and facilities, were getting far ahead of the sleepy irritating railways. Six years later, in 1936, the LNER sold the bus company some houses in Station Parade which were demolished to make way for a bus station.

On 15th July 1907 the NER had begun char-a-banc trips from Harrogate to such destinations as Fountains Abbey, Bolton Abbey and Ripley. Later destinations such as Richmond and Aysgarth Falls were added. The local press thought a more atrocious and dangerous nuisance than "these beastly smelling machines" was not known. Nidderdale folk considered them too wide for the narrow dales roads but did not want the roads widening and the dales made accessible to even larger vehicles. The excursions from Harrogate ceased on the outbreak of war in 1914 and never resumed.

EXHIBITIONS AND SPECIAL TRAINS

On 26th October 1917 an ambulance train for the use of wounded troops in France was exhibited in Bower Road goods yard. Despite very bad weather it attracted 2,551 visitors who paid £146 0s 6d to the Red Cross in admission charges. The previous April an egg and poultry demonstration train had attracted 1,360 people to Harrogate station.

Throughout the inter-war years the Corporation and the LNER worked together in publicising the town. In 1932 of £5,000 spent annually on advertising Harrogate half was contributed by the LNER. In 1934 "tourist" carriages were exhibited at Harrogate station. In March 1935 Class D49, 4-4-0, No. 234 "Yorkshire" spent a fortnight at Harrogate on exhibition with sleeping cars, camping coaches, demonstration vans and a cinema car. In 1938 "tourist" carriages were again exhibited and a cinema car showed colour films of the area served by the railway. Also in 1938 the "Stirling Single", 4-2-2, No 1, spent two days on show at Harrogate with a train representing the "Flying Scotsman" of 1888.

In 1930 crowds flocked to Harrogate station to watch the passage of the 4-6-4 "Hush Hush" loco, No. 10000, which was undergoing trials between Darlington and Leeds. Later this loco could often be seen working the "Queen of Scots" through the town.

Diesel electric loco No.10800 worked a special between Lincoln and Harrogate, via Church Fenton, in 1957. New "Metrovick" diesel - electric locos ran through Ripon, Harrogate and Wetherby in 1958 while on test, and in 1959 "Baby Deltic" diesel loco, No. D5902, was exhibited at Harrogate station.

In May 1962 Schools Class No. 30925 "Cheltenham" and Class 2P, 4-4-0, No. 40646, double headed an enthusiasts special from Nottingham to Darlington, via Church Fenton, Wetherby, Harrogate, Starbeck and Ripon. Two years later, in October 1964, preserved locos No. 4472

Plate 4.3   Old express engines demoted from express train duties on the East Coast Main Line were transferred and could often be seen performing more menial tasks. Here, a NER Fletcher design 2-4-0 of class 1440, No. 364, is shunting stock in the middle carriage siding alongside the main southbound platform under the station footbridge in August 1919. This class of locomotive had been demoted to lighter local passenger duties back in the late 1880's upon the introduction of more powerful 4-4-0 engines. M.Grocock collection.

Plate 4.4   A Great Northern Railway small boiler Atlantic arrives in Harrogate with a train of clerestory bogie stock on a through service from Kings Cross to Edinburgh. Introduced in 1902 these trains were routed via Doncaster, Knottingley and Church Fenton. Note the number of porters lined up awaiting the arrival of this train.   G. Pierson collection.

Plate 4.5   NER class Q1 4-4-0 No.1870 (built 1896, withdrawn 1930) is seen in Harrogate station with a northbound train including a horsebox behind the locomotive.   Note the NER coach No.440, a NER diagram 7 luggage composite built in 1897, standing in platform 6 behind the locomotive. This engine and No. 1869 were notable for having the largest coupled wheels in the world at 7ft 7¼in. Whilst specially designed for working fast trains on the East Coast Main Line both engines were stabled at Neville Hill, Leeds by 1907.   G. Pierson collection.

Plate 4.6   Spotless GNR Ivatt class D1 4-4-0, No. 1372, stands in No.1 Platform at Harrogate with a short train of GNR clerestory coaches. Platforms 1 and 2 were built in the late 1890's with fully glazed awnings.   G.Pierson collection.

"Flying Scotsman" and No. 3442 "The Great Marquess", after arriving at Harrogate with special trains, double-headed a combined train to Darlington, via Ripon. To mark the event commemorative platform tickets were sold at Harrogate. Steam locos disappeared from the Harrogate area in 1967 and from BR in 1968, but in September 1975 Midland Railway 4-4-0, No 1000 was exhibited in Harrogate station and the following year returned with ex LNWR 2-4-0, "Hardwicke" on a special train from York to Carnforth. In the summers of 1978 and 1979 a regular steam service was run each Sunday on a circular route from York to York, via Harrogate and Leeds. In 1982 it was decided the steam hauled "Scarborough Spa Express", introduced the previous year between York and Scarborough, would be extended to serve Harrogate and Leeds. Unfortunately by the end of the 1980s this service had ceased.

ROYAL VISITS

On 21st August 1902 a record number of tickets to Starbeck were sold at Harrogate. The buyers, however, only wanted to gain access to Harrogate station platforms to glimpse the Prince of Wales on his way to Studley Royal in a royal saloon attached to the 1.40 pm from Kings Cross. This train was hauled by GNR, 4-4-0, No. 1329.

When Princess Mary married in 1922 she took up residence, first at Goldsborough Hall, and later at Harewood House, often being visited by her mother, Queen Mary. In 1924 Queen Mary, and her husband, King George V, arrived at Harrogate in a royal saloon attached to the "Harrogate Pullman" and went by car to Goldsborough. On 26th August 1927 the Queen arrived at Harrogate in a royal saloon attached to the "Harrogate Pullman" which was hauled non-stop from Kings Cross by Class A1 Pacific, No. 2561 "Minoru". A more famous loco, No. 4472 "Flying Scotsman," brought the King and Queen to Harrogate on 21st August 1933 when their majesties arrived in a nine coach royal train. On her 1934, 1935 and 1936 visits Queen Mary arrived in Harrogate in royal saloon 395, attached to the 1.40 pm from Kings Cross. In 1934 the train was double-headed between Doncaster and Harrogate, via Church Fenton, by a Class D49, 4-4-0, and a Class D20, 4-4-0, and in 1936 by a Class D49, 4-4-0, and a Class D21, 4-4-0. In 1936 the Queen returned to London in royal saloon 395 attached to the "Yorkshire Pullman", which ran via the Starbeck - Pannal line instead of via Crimple Jct., its usual route. On 12th September 1938 Her Majesty arrived at Harrogate from Scotland in royal saloon 395 attached to the "Queen of Scots", which used the down platform and was headed by Class A4 Pacific No. 2511 "Silver King". She left on 19th September on the "Yorkshire Pullman" which ran via York, its usual route at that time, and was hauled by Class A4 Pacific No.4498 "Sir Nigel Gresley"

On 10th July 1957 the present Queen, and Prince Philip, travelled from Catterick Bridge to Harrogate, via Ripon, in the Royal Train, hauled by two Class B1, 4-6-0s, Nos. 61176 and 61224. After visiting the Great Yorkshire Show the royal party rejoined the train and proceeded to York hauled by two green liveried Class V2 2-6-2s.

The Queen visited Harrogate twice in 1985, once on 4th April when the Royal Train was hauled by No. 47 484 Ismabard Kingdom Brunel and again on 8th December when the Royal Train was hauled by No. 47 455.

ACCIDENTS AT HARROGATE STATION

On 10th August 1871 two empty carriages being shunted at Harrogate ran away down the incline towards Bilton. Near Dragon Jct. they caught a platelayer walking home along the line with his wife and dragged him three miles to Nidd Bridge. Here the stationmaster, informed by telegraph, ran the carriages into a siding. The badly injured platelayer was rushed to Leeds Infirmary by special train.

The northern end of the up platform at Harrogate station, for about 100 yards, was in 1888 a ticket platform. Here trains stopped for ticket examination before proceeding to the southern end to allow passengers to board or alight. To obviate the difficulty of restarting, if stopped on the rising gradient of 1 in 66 between Dragon Jct. and the station, trains were allowed to arrive at the ticket platform, even if the southern end of the up platform was occupied by another train, provided the Harrogate North signalman had satisfied himself the line was clear to the point the train had to run to. If he was in any doubt he had to stop the approaching train and caution the driver before he allowed it to enter the station. The driver had then to approach the station with special care. On 28th April 1888 the 3.50 pm Newcastle - Liverpool express was at the up platform, with the last of its 11 vehicles occupying part of the ticket platform, when it was struck in

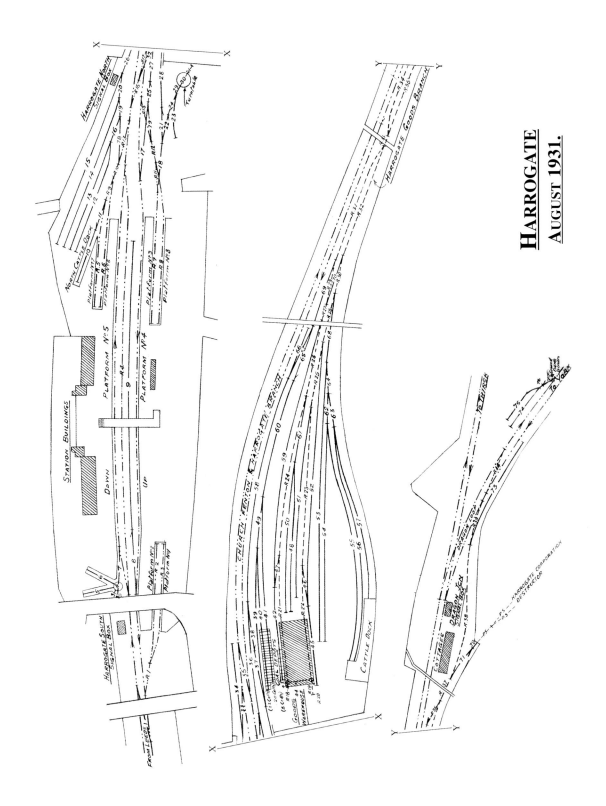

HARROGATE
AUGUST 1931.

the rear by the 6.10 pm from Pateley Bridge. There was no derailment but the rear buffers of the Liverpool train mounted those of the Pateley Bridge train. Seventeen passengers complained of injury. The blame was placed on the loco crew of the Pateley Bridge train, who had been on duty 12 hours, for failing to keep a proper look out, and on the Harrogate North signalman for not stopping their train and cautioning the driver.

There was also a ticket platform south of Station Bridge where down trains stopped for ticket examination before proceeding into the station. At one time there sat in a window overlooking the platform a parrot in a cage. The bird learnt to imitate the voices of railway staff and passengers and would cry "Tickets please" and "Oh I've lost my ticket". It even learnt to imitate the guards whistle but was removed when its language became too colourful.

On 5th September 1902 the 12 20 pm Edinburgh - Kings Cross was admitted to Harrogate station on the understanding a relief train was at the up platform. The loco crew however failed to keep a proper lockout and ran their train into the rear of the relief. Fortunately the slow speed of the London train meant little damage was done and no one seriously injured.

On 31st January 1925 the 9.00 am Ripon - Kings Cross express ran into the rear of the 9.25 am Harrogate - Bradford which was starting from Harrogate station. Although the Bradford train was well filled the rear coach, which was severely damaged, was almost empty and no one was seriously injured.

On 14th July 1927 an empty carriage being shunted at Harrogate ran away towards Leeds. Class D21, 4-4-0, No. 1241 gave chase and as Crimple Jct. approached a shunter on the front of the loco used his pole to couple the runaway to the loco. The brakes were applied and the carriage brought safely back to Harrogate.

On 11th March 1937 two empty coaches being shunted into a bay at Harrogate station by Class D17, 4-4-0, No. 1908, struck the buffer stops with such force a bogie was knocked off.

On 7th August 1956 a loco left Harrogate station for Starbeck shed. Unfortunately the route had not been set by the signalman resulting in the loco running into a siding knocking an empty coach through the buffer stops and into the window of a house in Nidd Vale Terrace. Fortunately no one was hurt.

THE CAT

Well known in the 1930s was the station cat. "The Cat", who had no name and who was on the station payroll, being paid in milk, arrived in Harrogate in a theatrical scenery van from Cardiff and took up residence in a hole in the station wall. She was introduced to Queen Mary and appeared in the local newspapers, and the "LNER Magazine". Sadly she used up all her nine lives under a train in 1938, but not before she had added between 40 and 50 kittens to the feline population of the town, one of which was adopted by Lady Ackroyd of Grantley Hall.

THE GOODS YARD

In 1862 some Harrogatonians opposed a goods yard at the end of Chapel Street (now Oxford Street) because, "it would be detrimental to the industry of Harrogate and a nuisance to visitors and residents." Although another site was suggested, in Strawberry Dale, it was not until 18th July 1898 that a goods yard, in Bower Road, was opened in central Harrogate. Prior to this, after the closure of Brunswick station to goods, in about 1864, all Harrogate's goods traffic had been dealt with at Starbeck.

In September 1948 coal merchants complained coal arriving at Harrogate contained a good deal of stone and slate, which they dumped in the goods yard. Unfortunately so much accumulated a contractor had to be hired to remove it, leaving the coal merchants to complain not only did they have to pay for the so called coal's delivery but also for its removal.

Coal traffic to Harrogate ceased in May 1984 and the goods yard, which had been a public delivery siding for some time, closed in July 1984. A supermarket has since been built on the site.

Plate 4.7   Sentinel Railcars were introduced to the North East area of the LNER in the late 1920's in an attempt to reduce the train operating costs. No. 2133 'Cleveland' is seen here at the north end of platform 7. The railcars operated many of the local services, particularly the frequent Harrogate – Knaresborough shuttle.   Stephenson Locomotive Society.

Plate 4.8   BR Type 2 'Baby Deltic' No.5902 stands in platform 6 during 1959 after being specially brought up from London as part of a conference organised by CAV, the diesel engine injection specialists. These locomotives were not as successful as their more powerful Type 5 counterparts leading to their early withdrawal in 1969.   G.Pierson collection.

Plate 4.9 The RCTS 'Roses' railtour from Manchester comprised of two 2-car 'Cravens' DMUs stand on the middle through line in Harrogate station on 8th June 1958. Driving Motor Composite, No. 50804, in the foreground identify these DMUs as two of the fourteen power-twin units built in 1957 being allocated to Newton Heath depot, Manchester, at the time. J. Edgington.

Plate 4.10 An ex-NER class J25 0-6-0, No.1743, shunts private owner coal wagons in Harrogate Goods Yard before World War Two. At this time it was usual for roughly half the coal wagons present at Harrogate to be colliery owned, the others being NER/LNER slope sided hopper wagons. The coaches stabled on the right include a 52ft long clerestory Open Composite coach, No. 23411, which was used as a club saloon on the 8.40am Harrogate - Leeds train. A similar coach (1st class only) was used on the 8.30am Harrogate – Bradford service. G.Pierson collection.

Plate 4.11   With plenty of steam escaping Starbeck allocated LNER class D49 4-4-0, No. 62752, 'The Atherstone' climbs the last few yards of the 1 in 66 gradient into Harrogate station with a train of LNER Gresley and Thompson carriages. When erected in 1898 the signal gantry carried a forest of arms indicating routes to the north end platforms. In 1929 this gave way to a mechanical route indicator showing the platform number and just one signal together with Harrogate South's distant and a 'calling-on' arm. By the time this view was taken the platform number is given by a theatre route indicator to the right of the signal post.   Ken Hoole collection.

Plate 4.12   An English Electric Type 4 (later class 40) No. 346 approaches Dragon Junction with the 12 noon from Kings Cross (1S57 down) 'The Queen of Scots' Pullman on 10th December 1961. The train is comprised of six newly introduced Metropolitan-Cammell Pullmans except the vehicles at the ends which are brake second carriages dating from 1928. To the left of the train are the tracks of the Harrogate Goods Branch which lead off to the left to go round the rear of some NER cottages and Dragon Jct. signal box.   I.H.B. Lewis/Ken Hoole collection.

Plate 5.1   NER class Z Atlantic, No. 2196, stands at the head of an up Pullman service. The six 12-wheel Clayton design Pullmans appear in the post 1929 colour scheme making this more likely to be the Newcastle – London 'West Riding Pullman' sometime between 1929 and 1935. Ken Hoole collection.

Plate 5.2   LNER 'Hush-Hush' 4-cylinder compound 4-6-4, No. 10000, on the 4.17pm Newcastle – Liverpool express in May 1935. The locomotive had been completed at Darlington in December 1929 being equipped with a high pressure water tube type marine boiler made and fitted by Yarrow & Co. of Glasgow. The engine, painted grey in this view, was rebuilt with a conventional boiler in 1937 together with A4 style streamlining. At the time this engine worked the 11.2am Leeds – Newcastle (9.0am ex-Liverpool) returning with the train shown travelling via Sunderland in both directions. The train is mainly comprised of LNWR stock with an LMS restaurant car towards the centre.   G. Pierson collection.

Chapter 5

RIPON

When opened in 1848 Ripon station was considered to be temporary. In 1851 one passenger referred to the stopping place for trains, for he could not call it a station, as a miserable collection of wooden boards. There were also complaints that the down platform was unprotected from the weather. In 1852 the Editor of the "Harrogate Advertiser" complained the station staff at Ripon avoided giving assistance and information, but the main complaint of travellers was that the station was almost a mile from the city. Although a permanent station was later built it was built on the same site.

A loco shed was opened at Ripon when the line from Thirsk reached the city. This shed appears to have been closed when the line was extended to Leeds for in 1864 the NER abandoned plans to build one. In 1867 Ripon City Council expressed concern about the wooden viaduct across the Ure. The NER assured them it was safe but, nevertheless, replaced it with a more substantial structure the same year. This viaduct was demolished in 1972 after the line's closure.

In 1845 the L & T had bought the Ripon Canal to prevent its owners opposing the building of the railway through Ripon. Traffic on the canal declined once the railway opened and in 1894 the NER sought to abandon it. This was opposed by the city councils of Ripon and York. In desperation the NER offered to give the canal away, but no one would have it and it remained railway property until after nationalisation.

On 13th August 1904 the NER introduced a motor bus service between Ripon station, Ripon Market Place and, in summer, Studley Royal. On the first day many of the passengers were travelling to the Marquis of Ripon's garden party at Studley Royal. In 1905 a passenger reported the bus was elegantly furnished and, from the outside, very neat but vibration and noise somewhat detracted from its merits. The service from Ripon station ceased in July 1920.

During its life Ripon station saw a number of distinguished visitors. In September 1858 Queen Victoria travelled north after the opening of Leeds Town Hall. Over 6,000 people watched the Royal Train pass through Starbeck, but any glimpse of the Queen was brief. The crowd of almost 3,000 at Ripon were more fortunate for here the train stopped for five minutes. Admission to the down platform was by ticket only, but there was no restriction on admission to the up platform of the flower bedecked station, where the Queen acknowledged the cheers of the crowd.

Crowds at Ripon on 25th October 1887 witnessed the arrival by the 3.45 pm from Leeds of the former Prime Minister, Gladstone, who was to spend a few days at Studley Royal. The North Staffordshire Railway provided a special saloon for the journey and this was coupled to the 9.52 am Newcastle - Liverpool when Gladstone left for Hawarden on 28th October.

In 1895 the Prince of Wales visited Studley Royal. The Royal Train travelled from Kings Cross to Ripon via York and Starbeck and the next day ran from Ripon to Leeds, via the Bilton - Starbeck - Pannal line.

In April 1928 the Duke and Duchess of York arrived in Ripon on the "Queen of Scots" Pullman. The down "Queen of Scots", hauled by York Class A1 Pacific, No. 60146 "Peregrine", made a special stop at Ripon on 8th April 1953 for the Queen Mother to alight. Another unscheduled stop, this time involving the up "Queen of Scots", occurred on 10th May 1956 when York Class A2/3 Pacific, No.60524 "Herringbone", failed at Ripon. After an hour's delay the train was worked forward by two Starbeck Class J39, 0-6-0s, Nos.64821 and 64942.

A man was sent to prison for three years for stealing the purse of Mary Worsdell at Ripon station in 1860. Mrs Worsdell was the wife of Nathaniel Worsdell, who had built the tender for Stephenson's Rocket. She was also the mother of Thomas and Wilson Worsdell both later locomotive superintendents of the NER.

Ripon station, unfortunately, also saw a few accidents. On 6th February 1852 a goods train from Leeds was being reversed across the up line at Ripon to the goods shed when it was struck by a passenger train from Thirsk. Wagons were smashed and the loco of the passenger train damaged but no one was seriously injured. The "Leeds Mercury" thought the site of Ripon station about the worst that could have been selected because the curve and cutting to the north obstructed the view of drivers approaching from that direction.

A similar accident occurred on 2nd May 1867 when a passenger train from Stockton collided with a goods train being reversed across its path at Ripon. Again no one was seriously injured.

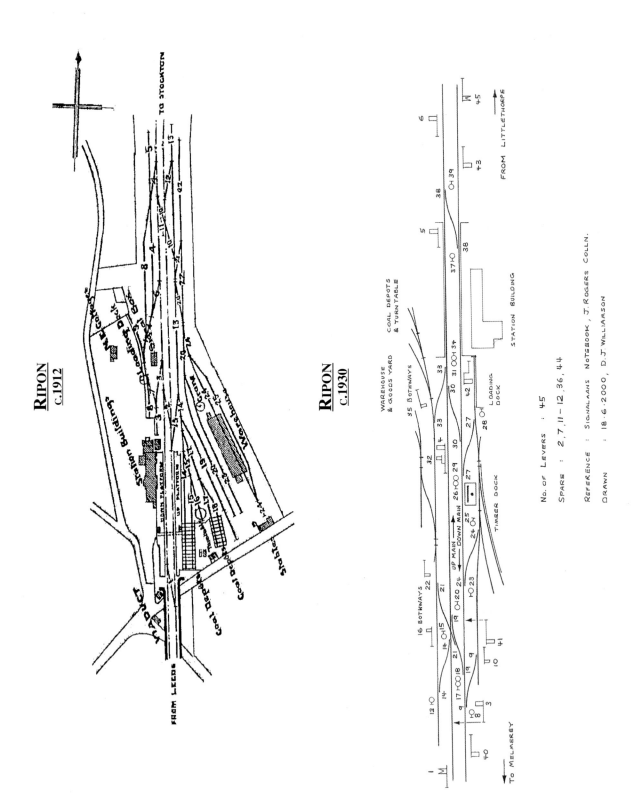

RIPON c.1912

RIPON c.1930

No. of Levers : 45

Spare : 2, 7, 11 – 12, 36, 44

Reference : Signalmans Notebook, J. Rogers Colln.

Drawn : 18·6·2000, D.J. Williamson

Plate 5.3   BR 350hp 0-6-0 shunter, No. 3239, is about to leave Ripon's up independent line on a goods bound for Starbeck on 8th August 1961. After the closure of Starbeck shed a diesel shunter was outstationed from York for local pilot duties around Harrogate. The up independent was one of a number of wartime improvements to capacity on this line made during 1942.   J.W.Hague/G.Pierson collection

Plate 5.4   The original Leeds & Thirsk station was quickly replaced by this structure opened in 1854 at a cost of £3840. The North Eastern Railway ran one of the first motor bus services between the station and Ripon Market Square - the siting of the Station, a mile or so out of the centre of town, did not help to attract passengers in later years. However Ripon was the nearest station to Fountains Abbey and at one time generated sufficient military traffic to justify a separate booking office. The main station buildings have more recently been turned into housing.   Ken Hoole collection.

In 1866 Mr Paddock, one of the managers of an exhibition entitled "The American Rebellion" which had been on exhibition at Ripon, went to the railway station to order a wagon to take the exhibition to Otley. He was directed to cross the line and proceed to the goods department but in the dark took a wrong turning and fell down the first shaft of the coal depot dislocating his arm and injuring his leg.

A northbound passenger train slowing to stop at Ripon on 18th July 1868 was passed by a southbound goods, the last wagon of which was on fire. Although flames passed through the open windows of the passenger train the passengers escaped unhurt. In another incident, in May 1910, fire broke out in a wagon of sleepers in a siding at Ripon and quickly spread to three more. The station master ordered the wagons be run under the water column used for replenishing the tanks of steam locos, drenched and the fire extinguished.

Around 10.00 pm on 11th September 1893 a Newcastle - Leeds provision train, which had passed a danger signal, ran into the rear of a mineral train in Ripon station. The loco of the Leeds train was derailed, the guard's van of the mineral train thrown onto a coal truck, two or three wagons smashed and the line blocked until 7.00 am the next day.

At Ripon the last railway horse was replaced by a motor vehicle in 1935. This change came too late for one Ripon railwayman who had died the previous year after being kicked by his horse when it was frightened by a steam lorry.

Ripon station stood intact for some years after closure but in 1990 the station building was converted into flats, and houses were built on the rest of the site. The goods shed and stables also still stand. Part of the Ripon by-pass now runs alongside part of the old railway's embankment on the south side of the River Ure.

MONKTON MOOR

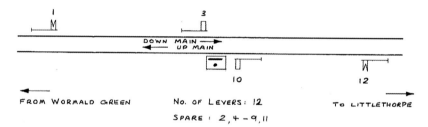

LITTLETHORPE

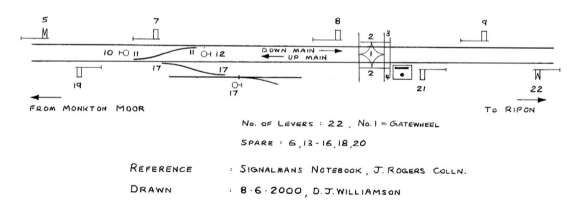

Plate 5.5 The 'Northern Belle' land cruise train stands at Ripon in the summer of 1934 - this was a prime example of LNER enterprise in promoting luxury rail travel 60 years before the modern day Orient Express. A powerful looking LNER Gresley design class K3, 2-6-0, No. 17 has been provided as motive power. The train started out from London behind a class A3 running as far as Wetherby where it stabled overnight - both day and night coaches were provided. The following morning the 17 coach train continued to Harrogate behind two class K3s. Passengers then travelled by road to Ripon where they rejoined the train before going on to tour various lines in the north of England and the Scottish Highlands.   RAS Marketing..

Plate 5.6 A panoramic view of Ripon goods yard and station viewed from the north.   Ripon had the most extensive goods facilities on the Leeds Northern apart from Starbeck. Between the goods shed on the left and the up side station buildings there were two sets of double track coal cells together with a small turntable provided to turn the engine operating the Masham branch. The signal box, dating from 1907, replaced two earlier boxes, Ripon South and North. Ken Hoole collection

Plate 6.1 An unidentified ex-NER Raven, class B16/1, 4-6-0 locomotive heads a special train for the Royal Canadian Mounted Police at Dragon Junction after a visit to the Great Yorkshire Show. The train is comprised of ex-LMS passenger coaches for the riders whilst the horses are accommodated in a mixture of LMS and BR horseboxes. The line to Bilton Junction can be seen falling away to the left whilst on the right the junction for the branch to Harrogate Goods Yard can be seen, complete with protecting signal and catchpoint.   H.Whitby/S.Askew collection.

Plate 6.2 LNER class J39 0-6-0, No. 64863 pilots an unidentified class WD 2-8-0 locomotive on a Teeside – West Riding goods train at Dragon Junction. The gradient on this line can be appreciated in this view compared with the Starbeck line on the right.   Ken Hoole collection.

Chapter 6

ACCIDENTS ON THE LEEDS NORTHERN

Since the coming of railways to Harrogate the local press has always been on hand to report the misfortunes that have happened, be they tragic, unlucky or hair-raising. The study of these early reports often brings out interesting details about the railway itself and the people who ran it.

The guard of a Ripon - Knaresborough - York passenger train was killed on 1st June 1853 when a loco wheel broke near Wormald Green. His funeral at Knaresborough was attended by stationmasters, drivers and over 40 guards from various companies, some of whom arrived by special train. In August 1853 a train ran into a cart on an occupation crossing between Weeton and Pannal. Two horses pulling the cart were killed and the farmer severely injured.

On 19th September 1854 defective workmanship during construction caused part of the roof of Bramhope Tunnel to collapse and a Leeds bound passenger train, hauled by two locos, ran into the rubble. Some carriages broke away and ran back down the incline but a guard, although badly injured, managed to stop them at Arthington. Here they were run into by another carriage that had followed them down. Several passengers were injured, but none fatally. The injured guard later received a substantial reward from grateful passengers. The tunnel was closed to goods trains until December and to passenger trains until 1st January 1855.

A young female mill worker named Lawrence arrived at Leeds Wellington Street station one night in October 1854. She had been drinking with another female and a man named Law. Seeing she was drunk the guard helped her buy a ticket for Horsforth and saw her safely into a third class carriage. As the train was about to depart Law took a seat in the same carriage without buying a ticket. On arrival at Horsforth the guard went to collect Law's fare but to his surprise found the carriage empty. The next morning Lawrence's mangled body was found on the line about a mile from Headingley station. Murder was suspected and Law was arrested. In his defence he said he had jumped from the train to avoid paying his fare leaving Lawrence safely in the carriage. The coroner's jury returned an open verdict and censored the guard for, knowing Lawrence was drunk, not checking the carriage each time the train stopped at a station. They also recommended offside carriage doors be locked in future.

Some carriages of a Leeds - Ripon train became detached at Headingley in 1858 and rolled back down the incline towards Leeds. Some passengers jumped out but the carriages were stopped before the Aire Viaduct was reached.

Railways proved unlucky for the Mountain family. In July 1847 a Staveley blacksmith named Mountain, employed on the railway near Brafferton, drowned whilst bathing in the River Swale. In November 1852 an excursion train returning from Northallerton races stopped at Melmerby. On alighting Joseph Mountain fell between the carriage and the platform and was killed when the train moved off. Another Mountain owned the "Greyhound Hotel" a coaching inn at Boroughbridge, whose trade was considerably reduced by the coming of the railways. One Mountain however remained in the coaching business. In 1858, when the watchman in the goods department at Melmerby was severely injured in a shunting accident, it was reported Mr Stirk, who drives Mr Mountains bus, took less than eight minutes to obtain medical aid. Until 1904 Mountains provided a bus service between Ripon station and the city centre.

An incident occurred at Pannal on 22nd May 1861, which caused a sensation at the time. At 9.10 pm a goods train left Thirsk for Leeds. It consisted of loco No. 374 and 32 wagons. Its driver was William Burton of New Wortley, Leeds, its fireman James King and its guard James Radley. It was a fine moonlit night. At Ripon they detached seven wagons and proceeded south at 10.00 pm, passing through Starbeck without stopping at 10.50 pm. As the train approached Pannal, 35 minutes late, at a speed under 20 mph, King felt a sudden click, as if something had broken and shouted to his driver, "She's off the road Bill". Burton did not reply but immediately shut off steam. The engine continued bouncing up and down and then turned over on to its right side on to the embankment with its tender completely turned round by the force of the derailment, and with the leading four wagons, loaded with coke, piled up on the engine and tender. Two wagons loaded with wheat fouled the down line and the track was severely damaged for some distance. King felt steam blow on him and something struck him in the back, but he managed to jump on the engine's running plate, and from there leapt on to the embankment. He looked for his driver, who was trapped under the wreckage, and shouted to the guard for help. Radley who had been thrown from his seat to the other side of his van by the derailment, came and gave him his lamp but said he must first prevent a goods train from Stockton running into the rear of the wrecked goods train. King, although injured, then crawled in to the wreckage and found Burton, badly injured, near the locomotive's regulator. He pulled him out and left him on the embankment while he went to Pannal for assistance. Near Pannal he came to three cottages occupied by railwaymen. It was now about 11.15 pm. On knocking at the first two doors he received no reply but the third was answered by a Mrs Crowder, wife of James Crowder, a plate-layer. Being so late at night she was suspicious and at first did not believe King. She was about to shut the door but he pleaded, "Oh missus I'm not making game, I believe my mate is dying". She then went to the other cottages to arouse their occupants whilst King proceeded to Pannal station. In the meantime Radley had walked 800 yards to the rear of his train and placed a lamp he had taken from his van in the middle of the track. He also placed fog signals on the line to warn the following goods train. On returning to the wrecked train he found Burton lying on the embankment. Burton told him his arm hurt but Radley said he could do him no good but would go to Pannal for assistance. At Pannal he met King and the stationmaster, George Crowe. There was some confusion as to whether the signals were lit or not and in the end a platelayer was sent to light them. The stationmaster appeared not to know what to do. On being told the driver was badly injured all he could say was, "Oh dear, oh dear, there is not a doctor within two miles", and suggested Radley saddle a horse and fetch one. Radley instead took some gin from the station and went to give it to Burton whilst Crowe went to Spacey Houses for help. Eventually a train came and took Burton and King to Leeds. A stop was made at Arthington, where brandy was obtained, but before Horsforth was reached Burton died. He was 27 years old.

The derailment was caused by a wheelset of a platelayer's trolley being placed across the line in a deliberate attempt to derail a train. This had been done sometime after 9.00 pm when the last train prior to the derailed goods had passed. The trolley had been used by platelayers that day but on finishing work, around 4.30 pm, they had dismantled it and placed the wheelsets six feet away from the track and below its level. It was therefore impossible for the wheelset to have found its way back onto the track without human agency. At the inquest it was stated that as far as was known no one had a grudge against the Railway Company, or any of its drivers. Mrs Trees, wife of William Trees, landlord of the "Old Spacey Houses" public house, said they had been no strangers in the house the night of on the derailment.

All railwaymen employed at Pannal were present on the night of the derailment and all were sober. Suspicion however fell on Thomas Richmond, a railway labourer of Pannal, who was arrested but released when no evidence against him could be found. Two weeks before the derail-ment he had been drunk and had struck station master Crowe. In reply Crowe had knocked him to the ground. Richmond said that by the 22nd all had been forgotten and he and Crowe were now friends. Crowe confirmed this and said he considered Richmond the last person to deliber-ately derail a train. Richmond, who had not worked on the 22nd because he said he could not get the wage he wanted, said he had been with Mary Wilkinson at Kirkby Overblow until 9.00 pm. He had then spent the rest of the evening at the "Shoulder of Mutton" at that place and returned home about 10.00 pm. This was confirmed by his mother and his brother. However George Hardy, a Kirkby Overblow tailor, said he had met Richmond in a field about 20 minutes walk from Spacey Houses, and about 15 minutes walk from the scene of the derailment, at about 10.30 pm on the night of the derailment when they had discussed Kirkby Feast. At the inquest Richmond stated he believed it was near 10.00 pm when he arrived home. He would not swear it was before 10.15 pm but he would swear it was before 11.00 pm. He did not remember meet-ing Hardy but would not swear he didn't. The coroner commented on the improper way Richmond gave evidence. Whatever he said, as soon as he was confronted with evidence to the contrary, he would not swear he was right but simply say he could not remember. Whether this was from ignorance or design the coroner said it was not for him to say but his evidence was most unsatisfactory.

The coroner's jury visited the scene of the derailment by special train and later returned a ver-dict of wilful murder by a person, or persons, unknown. The NER offered a £100 reward. It was also said the Home Secretary would not only be asked to increase this but would ask Queen Victoria to grant a free pardon to any accomplice, not being the main party involved, who would give evidence leading to a conviction.

Six years later, in December 1867, the Pannal derailment was being discussed in the "Traveller's Rest" in Burley, near Leeds, when a man named John Steel was overheard to say if he was to tell all he knew he would have to answer for it, although he was 20 miles away at the time. He added the men involved, one of whom was a coachman, had no grudge against the loco

The Leeds Northern bridged the River Nidd between Bilton Junction and Ripley Junction. Nidd Viaduct has 7 stone arches rising to a maximum height of 50 feet. This June 1991 view of the reflected arches shows how trees have grown to emphasise the narrow river valley. C.E.Williamson.

NER Worsdell class R1 4-4-0, No. 1238, emerges from the north portal of Bramhope Tunnel in this postcard view. Ten class R1s were built in 1908-9 at Darlington works. Although impressive in appearance their large grate made them somewhat hungry for coal. When new they were allocated to Neville Hill and York sheds for main line express workings. M.Grocock collection.

At Weeton the original station buildings situated by the main Harrogate – Pool road were superseded in NER days in favour of a booking office and other facilities at platform level. These buildings were then turned into cottages for railway employees. June 1991. C.E.Williamson.

LNER Class D49/2, No. 62745, 'The Hurworth' crosses Wharfe Viaduct with a Leeds – Ripon local train in June 1957. This viaduct, just to the north of Arthington village, spans the Wharfe Valley on a graceful curve of 21 sandstone arches rising to some 60 feet above the blue River Wharfe. Colour-Rail BR1472.

LNER Thompson class K1 2-6-0, No. 62007, enters Pateley Bridge in the early 1960s with the pick-up goods past the long closed signal box. The River Nidd flows close to the branch at this point.   Colour-Rail.

Ex-works class A6, 4-6-2T, No. 69791 stands on Starbeck shed in June 1950. Designed by Wilson Worsdell as a class W 4-6-0T in 1907 but rebuilt in 1917 these engines were allocated to Starbeck for banking freight trains from Bilton Junction up through Harrogate and on to Wetherby. One of the four locomotives of its class allocated to Starbeck at this time, No. 69791 was withdrawn in August 1951. Colour-Rail BR479.

Colour slides of Harrogate station are rare, pre-war views are rarer still. Here ex-NER Worsdell class D17/2, No.1873 is pictured in platform 5 during 1937. 1873 was withdrawn in February 1948. Colour-Rail NE176.

The up 'Queen of Scots' Pullman hauled by LNER Gresley class A3 4-6-2, No. 60081 'Shotover' has past Arthington North Junction and comes through the station in June 1957 on its way to Leeds Central. There a fresh engine would come on to the rear of the train to haul it on to London Kings Cross. Gresley class A3s or Peppercorn class A1s were the favoured motive power during the 1950s on this service. Colour-Rail BRE1442

No. 1242 of class D21 (NER class R1) stands outside the north end of the two road Starbeck shed in 1937. Though the engine is painted in lined black livery this is not very evident beneath the grime. Nos.1241 and 1242 had been allocated to Starbeck by April 1931 but by 1935 their numbers had been swelled by the addition of 1245 and 1246. Their rosters included Harrogate – London King Cross trains to Leeds as well as other semi-fast on the Leeds Northern. No. 1242 was withdrawn in January 1946 from Neville Hill shed. Colour-Rail NE182

driver and it had been done in a drunken spree. He was arrested but released when no further information, or evidence, could be obtained and the person, or persons, responsible for the derailment were never caught.

Guard Radley had been less than impressed by Crowe's actions on the night of the derailment. He told the inquest that Crowe appeared "stagnated and put out". The coroner remarked that with the exception of Crowe, who appeared to have been very faint hearted, the company's servants had done all in their power on the night. Crowe's reward appears to have been the sack for by September 1861 Pannal had a new stationmaster, Samuel Green. On the 24th of that month Crowe was fined £1 with costs for wilfully obstructing him. Crowe had been found in a second class carriage without a ticket and Green "got him out quickly". That evening Crowe went to Pannal station to enquire if something had come for him. When told it had not he became violent, rushed in to the office and struck Green in the face. Other blows were tried but Green defended himself and threw Crowe out. Crowe was in trouble again two months later in November 1861. Arriving at Pannal by the 6.18 pm train he gave up his ticket but used a variety of bad language and refused to leave the station. He eventually left when a policeman was called but was heard to say he would kill Green. He was later bound over for six months in the sum of £20.

By 1868 Pannal had a new stationmaster, Vincent Lawton. In 1870 he appeared in court charged with embezzling sums totalling £71 3s 3d from the NER. Surprisingly the NER police superintendent told the court his instructions were not to press the charge as they did not wish to act with any vindictive feeling towards the prisoner but left the matter in the hands of the justices. The justices, however, considered the matter serious. Lawton pleaded guilty and was sentenced to six months imprisonment.

On 6th June 1861, two weeks after the Pannal derailment, the driver of a passenger train approaching Newby Wiske about 8.30 pm felt his engine bounce and oscillate in an unusual manner. Believing a rail had been displaced he noted the spot, stopped his train at the next gatehouse and informed its occupant. The gateman on proceeding to the spot found several crushed stones on the rails. An NER detective was notified and soon apprehended two boys from Maunby who admitted placing stones on the line. In court it was decided they had acted out of childish mischief rather than malice and they were discharged. The bench, however, suggested their parents flog them on their return home.

On 20th October 1863 the loco of a Leeds - Pateley Bridge goods, having taken water at Arthington, was returning to its train when its boiler exploded. The goods shed was damaged and the back of the passenger shed blown into fields behind. The telegraph office, adjoining the passenger shed, was also damaged and a spring from the loco thrown into a nearby field. A porter, and a mother, and her two year old daughter, waiting in the passenger shed, were scalded, the child fatally. The stationmaster's son, who was in the goods shed, was severely scalded and a

Plate 6.3 When the LNER closed Pannal Junction signal box in 1927 the points were thereafter electrically operated from the station box at Pannal. On 20th July 1944 they failed to close properly and caused the derailment of ex-NER Atlantic No. 720 hauling the 12.57pm Leeds to Harrogate train. The locomotive fell onto its right hand side whilst damaged was sustained to the first three coaches of the train. Note how the derailment has also caused the signal arm to become disconnected and drop out of sight. Ken Hoole collection.

man with him struck by small fragments and slightly scalded. The loco crew, surprisingly, escaped unhurt. A passenger train had left three minutes before, otherwise the accident might have been worse. The down line was blocked by debris for three hours.

In August 1866 a man was seriously injured after falling from a train near Wormald Green, and in August 1884 the body of a man, who had fallen from a train the night before, was found by the Rigton signalman near Weeton.

A Leeds to Thirsk goods was run into by the 6.20 pm Stockton - Leeds passenger train at Arthington on 19th December 1868. The speed of the passenger train was only 5 mph consequently little damage was done.

On 17th December 1869 a goods train from Leeds, unable to stop because of mechanical failure, ran into another reversing into sidings at Pannal. Both locos were derailed and the line blocked for six hours.

In 1871 a northbound passenger train was derailed shortly after leaving Bramhope Tunnel but no one was seriously injured. In February 1865 a line was opened between Arthington and Otley. A new Arthington station was built at the south junction of the triangle formed at Arthington and the old Arthington station, situated where the Arthington - Pool road passes under the railway, was closed. The new station was meant to be temporary, until the ground settled, but it was not until 1873 that a permanent station was built. This was severely damaged by fire in 1895. In 1871 the NER refused permission for a footpath, to be built by public subscription, along the Wharfe Viaduct. The viaduct was often used illicitly as a means of crossing the river, consequently a watchman was employed to prevent trespassers. On 5th November 1872 the 8.35 pm Leeds - Thirsk passenger train, travelling at about 20 mph, struck a coal wagon standing foul of the main line. Wheels torn off the wagon caused the loco to derail and twist round. It then fell onto the wooden former booking office on the down platform of the old Arthington station, which had been converted into a home for the watchman and his family. The watchman was killed, his wife injured but their son escaped unhurt. The loco, after falling through the floor, came to rest upside down in the basement of the watchman's home, which rested on the slope of an embankment. The loco's tender ran on and struck the bridge over the Arthington - Pool road. Three carriages and a guard's van were also derailed but, with the exception of the van, which leaned over slightly, came to rest upright. The remainder of the train, three carriages, a horsebox and two guard's vans remained on the rails. The loco driver escaped with a few cuts and bruises. His fireman was thrown clear but could not remember precisely how, where or when. A bonfire night party had been in progress nearby. This led the inquest jury to believe the chock, which should have held the wagon in the siding, had been mischievously removed and they censured the NER for not providing a better means of securing the wagon. The Board of Trade, however, thought it unlikely the chock could have been removed without the culprit being seen and the cause of the accident remains a mystery.

The failure of facing points at Pannal Jct. to close properly caused the derailment of the 5.30 pm from Leeds on 25th January 1872. The loco fell onto its right side in the V of the junction and all nine vehicles in the train were derailed. The first vehicle, a first class carriage, fell onto its left side blocking the Starbeck lines. None of the passengers, amongst whom was the Bishop of Ripon, were seriously injured.

On 21st August 1872 the 8.00 pm Ripon - Leeds passenger train passed a signal at danger and struck the rear of the 3.00 pm West Hartlepool - Leeds goods, which was setting back onto the down line at Wormald Green to allow it to pass. The guard's van and seven wagons, out of 30 in the goods train, were derailed. Although the passenger train remained on the rails 21 passengers were injured. At that time, with the exception of special trains, approximately 43 trains in each direction passed through Wormald Green daily.

During foggy weather on 26th September 1873 the 5.55 am West Hartlepool - Leeds passenger train, travelling at a speed estimated at between 10 and 15 mph, ran into the rear of a Darlington - Leeds goods train which had been left on the main line at Arthington while its loco shunted. The loco of the passenger train was derailed, its smokebox door stove-in, its chimney knocked off and its buffer beam damaged. It's tender and train, however, remained on the rails and suffered little damage. Nevertheless 17 passengers were injured. The guard's van and three wagons at the rear of the goods were smashed but the other 29 wagons in the train were undamaged. An obsolete signal at the south end of the Wharfe Viaduct had led the driver of the passenger train into thinking the line was clear.

On 11th November 1873 the 11.35 am Harrogate - Leeds passenger train, travelling at about 12 mph, ran into the rear of a goods train left on the main line at Headingley while its engine shunted. A van and two wagons of the goods were badly damaged and 14 passengers injured. A signalling fault was to blame but the Board of Trade inspector also considered one brake van, and the tender brake, inadequate to stop ten vehicles running down a long incline such as existed at Headingley. Also he thought the driver of the passenger train might have kept a better look out.

A Spofforth man named Smith was killed on the line midway between Crimple Viaduct and Harrogate station in 1874. He was a trainee signalman and having missed his train at Pannal set off with his wife to walk along the line. They had crossed the viaduct and were nearing Harrogate when Smith noticed a southbound train. He put his wife safely on the side of the line but failed to notice a northbound train which struck him. On arrival at Harrogate the loco driver informed the authorities who immediately despatched an engine and carriage to bring the injured man to the station, but he died shortly afterwards.

On the evening of 27th November 1876 the 5.00 pm Leeds - Ilkley, via Arthington, ran into a herd of cows crossing the line where Burley Park station now stands. The engine was slightly damaged but no passengers were injured.

Early on 3rd January 1881 a northbound goods was passing Wormald Green when 11 wagons became derailed. The track was severely damaged and salt from wagons scattered over a wide area. Repairs occupied most of the day, during which time single line working was in force.

Thirteen wagons of a northbound goods were derailed at Bilton Jct. on 12th September 1881 badly damaging the track. The up line was soon cleared but the down was blocked for nine hours. Again large quantities of salt littered the area.

At about 6.03 pm on 24th October 1881 a Newcastle - Leeds, via Starbeck, goods stopped at a danger signal at Pannal Jct. Although the train had not passed the signal the signal's position was such that if a train came up to it the Pannal - Crimple line was fouled. The driver put his train into reverse but before movement occurred the double headed 5.30 pm Leeds - Newcastle express, running under clear signals, ran into it. Fortunately the 5.30 pm had reduced its speed to 35 mph ready to take the Crimple curve and the impact was lessened. The pilot loco fell onto its left side after hitting the loco of the goods. The train engine, with the coupling between it and the pilot broken, became derailed but ran on for 20 to 30 yards before falling onto its right side. Its tender came to rest upside down with the first vehicle of the express, a passenger van, on top. Out of nine vehicles in the express seven were derailed and some telescoped. Two farm workers ran to give assistance and freed one driver from beneath his loco when no one dared go near for fear of the boiler exploding. Two doctors on the train also rendered assistance until further help arrived from Harrogate. Miraculously no one was killed. The local press wondered how anyone

Plate 6.4   The end came prematurely for class D49, No. 62768 'The Morpeth' of Starbeck shed when it was in collision with two other locomotives of the same class at Dragon Junction in October 1952. This engine had been rebuilt by Thompson with inside cylinders in 1942. Instead of repairing the locomotive the buckled front frames spelt the end of this 4-4-0 seen here standing at Darlington. It was officially withdrawn on 3rd November 1952. J.W. Armstrong Trust.

escaped so completely was the front of the train wrecked. The engines, or what was left of them, fouled the up line and in all directions twisted metal and splintered wood bore evidence of the terrible force of the collision. Not only were sleepers torn up for a great distance but wheels were bent into all sorts of fantastic shapes. Three gangs worked throughout the night and by 9.00 am one line to Starbeck was open, but it was not until 4.00 pm that all lines were cleared and traffic working as normal. The Board of Trade inspector placed the blame on the driver of the goods for moving forward in anticipation of the danger signal changing before he reached it and so fouling the Pannal - Crimple line. However he added if all traffic past Pannal Jct. had been worked on the absolute block system, and two trains not been permitted to approach the junction at the same time, the accident would not have occurred. The public, however, believed the real cause of the accident was the position of the signal, which required a driver approaching it from Starbeck to stop 40 or 50 yards before he reached it. In fog or snow how was a driver to know how far he was from the signal? One man had heard regular drivers knew to stop when they reached a large bush growing by the lineside. If this was so then the bush was responsible for saving the lives and limbs of numerous Harrogate passengers and ought to be potted and placed in the Town Hall in commemoration of the fact. What was needed was a signal on the Starbeck side of Pannal Jct. to tell a driver, before he drove onto the junction, to either stop or proceed. In reply the NER stated they were altering all their junctions and hoped to have all their passenger lines worked on the absolute block system. This system was already in use on the Leeds - Harrogate line but not on that between Pannal and Starbeck.

At Arthington, on 1st March 1882, the loco of a Leeds - Newcastle goods was run into by its own train, which had become detached. The loco and several wagons were derailed blocking both lines.

John Scott, the organist and choirmaster of St Peter's church, Harrogate, was killed on the level crossing at Bilton on 6th March 1890. He had been giving music lessons at Bilton Dene and was returning on foot to Harrogate. He passed through a wicket gate at the crossing when a train from Harrogate came round the bend and ran him down.

The tender and leading vehicle of the 2.15 pm Harrogate - Leeds express became derailed as the train crossed the bridge over the Arthington - Pool road at Arthington on 22nd September 1898. The driver immediately stopping the train prevented the accident from becoming more serious, nevertheless both lines were blocked.

After leaving Starbeck northbound goods trains were sometimes halted by signals before Bilton Jct. Whilst waiting they often blocked a public footpath across the line. Impatient pedestrians would crawl under the train, and some in so doing would mischievously uncouple part of the train. On 9th March 1903 the driver of a Thirsk - Starbeck goods found a man's body near the crossing. It was assumed he had been crawling under the 11.25 am Starbeck - Middlesbrough goods and had been killed when it moved off. A similar crossing at Dragon Jct. was replaced by a footbridge after a mother and three year old daughter were killed by the 5.00 pm Harrogate - York on 28th May 1903.

The body of the "housekeeper" of the Crimple Jct. signalman was found on the former YNMR Crimple viaduct on the morning of Sunday 19th February 1905. She had been drinking in Harrogate the previous night and had been struck by a train while walking home along the line drunk.

At Melmerby in March 1906 a child wriggled through the level crossing gates while they were closed to road traffic and was killed by a train. The coroner's jury heard the duties of the Melmerby signalman could not be described as arduous, because he dealt with only 50 trains in nine hours. However he could not see in both directions at once and with 50 children crossing the line on their way to and from school one might easily slip through.

The "Harrogate Advertiser" reported in April 1907 that the 6 o'clock express from Leeds had nearly reached Pannal when the engine collapsed, several parts having dropped out of place. There was an hour's delay while a fresh engine was obtained.

Two platelayers were killed by an L & Y express between Pannal and Weeton on 4th November 1907. A curve in the line, and the passage of a Leeds - Newcastle train, prevented the driver seeing the men, and the men from seeing his train, until too late.

In April 1910, as the 10.08 am Newcastle - Liverpool express was approaching the Wharfe Viaduct, a pair of tender wheels became derailed. The train ran on over the viaduct damaging the track, until stopped near Arthington.

On 1st July 1914 a storm caused part of a cutting wall south of Harrogate to collapse. A large quantity of earth slid onto the line as the 1.40 pm Kings Cross - Harrogate was approaching but the driver managed to stop.

Two coaches were derailed as the 4.35 pm Leeds - Harrogate rounded the curve at Crimple Jct. on 26th April 1925 but no one was hurt. The curve at Crimple Jct. was also the scene of fatal accident on 7th August 1936 when the 8.57 am Bradford - Harrogate struck a cart on an occupation crossing. The four men in the cart, two of whom were killed, had failed to hear a warning shouted by the Crimple signalman.

The points at Pannal Jct. failed to close properly on 20th July 1944 and caused the derailment of the 12.57 pm Leeds - Harrogate passenger train. Ex NER 'Atlantic' No.720, hauling the train, fell onto its right hand side and the leading vehicle, a fruit van, was smashed. The next two vehicles, passenger coaches, were derailed but no one was seriously injured.

The line between Dragon Jct. and Harrogate North was blocked after wagons broke away from a southbound goods on 15th September 1946 and were derailed by catch points. Traffic was diverted over the Starbeck - Pannal line.

At 4.20 pm on 10th October 1947 four wagons of the 1.50 pm Newport - Mottram goods, hauled by War Department 2-8-0, No.70839, were derailed at Dragon Jct. when a chain fell through a wagon floor and fouled points. Traffic was diverted over the Starbeck - Pannal line until 11.10 am the following day and a bus service provided between Starbeck and Harrogate. A curiosity was one of the derailed wagons ended up with all its wheels on the adjoining line.

On restarting from Dragon Jct. at 1.36 pm on 29th October 1948 a Newport – Mottram goods, double-headed by another War Department 2-8-0, No. 3054, and Class A6, 4-6-2T, No. 9792, broke in two. The guard's van and eight wagons ran back and were derailed by catch points. The line was blocked, for seven hours. Trains diverted over the Starbeck - Pannal line included the "Queen of Scots", which on this occasion stopped at Pannal for Harrogate passengers.

Two women were killed on the level crossing at Headingley on Good Friday 1949. At the inquest the Starbeck crew who had charge of the train, the 2.05 pm Harrogate - Leeds, were exonerated from blame. It was suggested a subway or bridge replace the level crossing. The increased recreational use of the land east of Headingley and the lack of visibility of oncoming trains for pedestrians at the crossing caused a subway to be built before the closure of Headingley signal box in November 1967.

On 20th March 1950 the rear of the 8.05 am Newport - Milford goods ran back over catch points between Dragon Jct. and Harrogate North. The guard's van and four wagons were derailed and blocked both lines. Traffic was once again diverted over the Starbeck – Pannal line. This line was used for the same reason on 1st December 1950 when a goods was derailed between Harrogate and Crimple. On this occasion the speed of trains using the line had not to exceed 5 mph. The line between Dragon Jct. and Harrogate was blocked on 3rd April 1956 when wagons were derailed by catch points. Single line working was in force from 9.30 pm until 11.0 am the following day.

On 28th December 1932 the hounds of the Bramham Moor hunt ran down the side of the cutting near Nab Bridge, between Weeton and Pannal, into the path of a train, which just managed to stop without injuring them. On 22nd December 1956 a car ran down the cutting side near the same spot and was hit by the 4.13 pm Leeds - Harrogate train, hauled by Class D49, 4-4-0, No. 62736 "The Bramham Moor".

Shortly after restarting from Bilton on 2nd March 1959 the 7.00 am Newport - Milford goods, hauled by War Department 2-8-0, No. 90462, slipped to a stand. Permission was given to set back to Bilton, where an assisting loco could be attached, but in doing so five wagons were derailed by catch points.

The sharp bends in the road either side of Nab Bridge were introduced by the L & T to make bridging the railway easier. Before the railway came the Harrogate - Bradford road at this point was straight. On 23rd April 1983 a van ran into the bridge parapet and dislodged some coping stones as a Kings Cross - Harrogate HST was passing underneath. The window of the leading cab of power car No. E43118 was smashed and the driver seriously injured. Fortunately he later recovered.

Plate 7.1 An ex-NER class G5 0-4-4T, No. 67337 on a two coach train of NER elliptical roofed coaches runs into Knaresborough past the distinctive six sided stone built signal box during the early 1950's. The signal box, thought to have been built in 1875, contains a twelve lever frame installed in 1950. Knaresborough viaduct is behind the engine and offers some excellent views of the River Nidd at this point.   Ken Hoole collection.

Plate 7.2   At the east end of Knaresborough station the tunnel starts immediately after the platforms. Looking through the tunnel towards Goods Junction the siding leading up to the coal depots can be seen. Note the NER bracket signal sandwiched in between the water tank and platform edge. Ken Hoole collection.

Chapter 7

THE HARROGATE - YORK LINE

The L & T directors had originally intended to terminate their branch from Starbeck to Knaresborough on the Starbeck side of the Nidd but on 16th July 1846 an Act was obtained which allowed the line to be extended across the river. The same day the promoters of the East & West Yorkshire Junction Railway (E & WYJR) obtained an Act to build a line from York to Knaresborough, where an end to end connection with the L & T would be made. The E & WYJR was let in two contracts, the Kirk Hammerton of approximately ten miles, and the Knaresborough of approximately four. Although the former was of relatively easy construction its first contractor went bankrupt. The contractors for the Knaresborough contract, which included the tunnel and viaduct in the town, were Wilson & Benson. In March 1847 the directors requested they discontinue blasting in the town and "proceed so as not to excite the fears and apprehensions of the inhabitants." The foundation stone of Knaresborough Viaduct was laid on 5th April 1847. All shops in the town were closed and a holiday atmosphere prevailed with flags flying, bells ringing, cannons firing and a band marching the streets. At 1.00 pm a procession, led by railway officials and local dignitaries, formed in the castle yard, moved off through the market place and down the high street to where the stone was to be laid. Here stood a platform for the ladies, who were admitted by ticket only, and for whom refreshments were provided. Good weather prevailed and after prayers a bottle containing newspapers and documents connected with the line, was placed in a recess and the foundation stone laid over it by J Dent, the E & WYJR Chairman, who received a commemorative trowel and mallet. The ceremony over guests had dinner at the "Crown Hotel" whilst the workmen attended their own dinner, paid for by the directors.

A local astrologer predicted disaster for the viaduct but this was dismissed as rambling nonsense. Nevertheless in March 1848, when the viaduct was nearing completion, cracks began to appear in its arches and the basements of the piers began to bulge. On 10th March the workmen were called off. The next day the centre pier collapsed and the viaduct fell. No one was injured but fallen masonry dammed the river flooding houses in Waterside, and numerous fish were killed by lime polluting the water. Poor workmanship and inferior materials caused the collapse and those who inspected the ruins wondered, not that the viaduct had fallen, but that it had stood at all. With the viaduct in ruins soil from a cutting on the Starbeck side of the Nidd could not be brought over the river where it was needed to form an embankment. The building of a temporary wooden viaduct was considered but not proceeded with. Without the embankment the line could not be brought into Knaresborough. Consequently when the line from York was opened, on 30th October 1848, it terminated at Haya Park Lane, about a mile from Knaresborough, where a temporary station was built by Faviell & Son for £363. The line might have opened earlier but when the railway inspector examined it, on 6th July 1848, he found all bridges completed, but in many places the up line not yet laid, and where it was a good deal of ballasting was still required. The down line was laid, but was in poor condition, having been roughly laid for the contractor's use. It required to be lifted and levelled and in many places brought into proper alignment. None of the station platforms had been built, the locomotive turntable was not in place and the junction with the York - Darlington line not laid. A further inspection, on 17th July, found the junction laid, but the signals connected with it incomplete. The YN & B, who were responsible for working the junction, promised to send a description of the signals, with a certificate of their completion, but by 26th July these had not been received. The inspector therefore refused permission for the line to be opened, stating he believed its opening would be attended with great danger to the public.

The incompleteness of the works however did not prevent the running of a free train from Knaresborough to an agricultural show in York on 13th July. On the same day the Kirk Hammerton contractor's men boarded a train which, with banners flying and music playing, took them from Poppleton to Knaresborough. On arrival they marched in procession to the "Kings Arms" and drank with great cheering "Success to the East & West Yorkshire Junction Railway". They then returned to Poppleton where more than 400 were treated to a substantial dinner and a liberal supply of ale.

The E & WYJR directors never intended to work their line themselves. In 1847 they had rejected an offer from the YN & B to work the line in favour of one from the L & T. The E &

WYJR and the L & T had five directors in common, had agreed to share the expense of the works at Knaresborough and had even obtained powers to amalgamate. Unfortunately by 1848 many L & T shareholders, disillusioned with unprofitable branch lines, considered the E & WYJR worthless, especially with the viaduct in ruins. They therefore refused to honour their pledge to work the line, and would not even pay their share of the expense incurred on the works at Knaresborough until compelled to do so by a Chancery suit in 1853. Angered the E & WYJR turned to the YN & B who commenced to work the line from its opening, although on terms less favourable to the E & WYJR than previously offered. By March 1849 the E & WYJR was in poor financial shape. In that month shareholders were told the line between Knaresborough and Starbeck was nearly discontinued for want of funds. In the tunnel at Knaresborough there remained about 24 yards to be excavated and bricked, whilst another 50 yards was partially excavated. At the York end, because of danger to property from landslips, 30 yards had had to be added to the tunnel's length and strong retaining walls built to hold back the cutting sides. From Haya Park Lane, for about 100 yards towards Knaresborough, the ground remained unbroken and the embankment leading to the town unfinished. The outlay on both contracts had far exceeded that estimated. In the opinion of a committee appointed to look into the line, the stations and gatehouses were unnecessarily ornamental and it was thought, considering the company's finances, and the needs of each station, buildings of a substantial and useful character might have been erected at half the cost. A number of accommodation bridges, not included in the estimates, had to be built and the committee felt landowners should have been satisfied with level crossings, after all Parliament had been happy for the Great North Road to be crossed on the level at Hopperton.

By August 1849 the tunnel at Knaresborough was finished and the contract to rebuild the viaduct re-let to Duckett & Stead. This did not please the original contractors who fenced off the works to prevent anyone taking possession, and threw the fallen rubble back into the river as fast as the new contractors men brought it out. Locals feared a fight but a thunderstorm dispersed the men leaving the original contractors still in possession. The viaduct was eventually rebuilt by Duckett & Stead. The last keystone was laid on 30th August 1850 after which the workmen were treated to dinner and next day played cricket with men from Lingerfield Quarry, which had supplied the stone for the viaduct. In April 1851 magistrates ordered the L & T to contribute to the repair of the road from this quarry to the works at Knaresborough before 23rd June or face a fine of £1 a day thereafter.

The track of the York - Haya Park Lane line had been handed over by the contractor in bad condition but by March 1850 it had been consolidated and future expenditure on it was expected to be considerably less. To economise passenger trains had been reduced from three to two a day, except on market day. The Sunday service was withdrawn. Following a disagreement the YN & B ceased to work the line and in June 1850 the Leeds firm of locomotive builders, E.B.

HOPPERTON

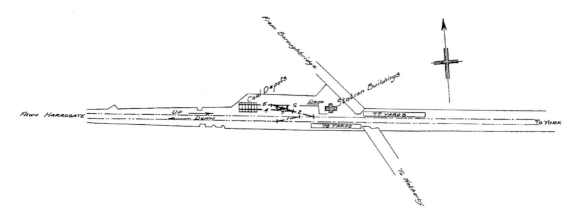

Plate 7.3   A Metro-Cammell 2 car DMU runs through Goldsborough station on the 1.25pm Harrogate – York working on 7th July 1959, whilst in the background LNER class J39 0-6-0, No. 64855 from Starbeck shed shunts the yard. The station building is hidden by the austerity pattern signal box which was built in connection with the Ministry of Food cold storage depot opened in 1942 seen here between the box and the DMU. D.J. Williamson collection.

Plate 7.4   The line between Knaresborough and Cattal was singled in December 1973. Here a Derby built class 108 DMU has just come off the single track section from Knaresborough into Cattal station on 23rd April 1987. The signalman returns to the cabin with the single line tablet. C.E. Williamson.

Wilson, took over. A new, lighter, more economical locomotive, the "Knaresborough" was set to work but matters were not improved by the YN & B demanding high tolls for the use of their line between Poppleton Jct. and York, and refusing to provide those facilities for handling traffic at York the E & WYJR directors considered their line was entitled to. In 1872 the Chairman of the NER said about 20 years previously he had frequently used the Knaresborough - York line. It then had only one locomotive which was made to do as much as possible hauling trains of passengers, goods and coal at an average speed of 4 mph. There was also only one set of carriages and trains were often stopped because the loco had broken down or its fire had gone out. He believed the line had been of little service to the public.

In January 1848 a man loading wagons with excavated soil in Raw Gap, Knaresborough had both legs broken by a fall of earth. This work was still proceeding in September 1850 when one man was killed and another injured by a fall of earth in Raw Gap.

The last stone in Knaresborough Viaduct was laid in February 1851. From 1st July that year the YNMR began working the E & WYJR and the following year the two companies amalgamated. The Haya Park Lane - Knaresborough section was opened on 21st July 1851, followed on 18th August by the Knaresborough - Starbeck section. In return for running powers between Knaresborough and Starbeck the YNMR withdrew passenger trains between Leeds and Harrogate, via Church Fenton. This agreement appears to have ceased by the end of 1851. After this the passenger service between Knaresborough and Starbeck became intermittent. The LNR had no interest in an unprofitable branch line and it was only in 1853 that a regular passenger service between the two places was reintroduced.

An interesting visitor to Harrogate in 1858 was Charles Dickens who hired a train to take him to York. It is not known for certain which station he used but it is believed to have been Starbeck. The York - Harrogate line was completed in 1862 when the NER built a line from Starbeck to its new station in central Harrogate.

In 1871 a passenger complained the platforms at Hessay and Hammerton, on the York line, and Arthington, on the Leeds line, were nearly a yard below the carriage floor with only one step between, "thus rendering it most inconvenient and even dangerous for aged persons and children and cannot be otherwise than painfully degrading to sensitive and modest women in every class." In 1880 a gale blew down a signalpost at Hammerton station. It also set in motion a wagon and propelled it, in which direction the report does not say, to the next station where its unexpected arrival without visible motive power caused some astonishment

In the same year Matthew Peacock, the Cattal stationmaster, was transferred to Ripon. On his departure he was presented with a silver tea service inscribed, "This silver tea service was present to Mr Matthew Peacock on his leaving Cattal station by a few friends in acknowledgement of his efficient and courteous conduct as station master during the period of 11 years."

Knaresborough station was rebuilt in 1865 but in 1887 Knaresborough town authorities asked for a waiting room on the down platform of Knaresborough station, a second class ladies waiting room, the enlargement of the company's offices and better provision for booking tickets. They also asked that an excursion train from the North to Harrogate be routed via Boroughbridge and Knaresborough and passengers be allowed to alight, or join, at those places. Also that all Sunday excursions from the West Riding to Harrogate be extended to Knaresborough or, failing this, passengers be allowed to alight at Starbeck and travel to Knaresborough by ordinary trains at no extra charge. The continuation, from Knaresborough to Boroughbridge, of the 3.05 pm arrival from Harrogate, and a train from Harrogate to Knaresborough between 7.42 pm and 10.00 pm was also requested. This latter request being made because between those times six trains from Leeds and elsewhere arrived in Harrogate. By January 1888 an additional train leaving Harrogate for Boroughbridge at 2.50 pm, and a train from Harrogate to Knaresborough at 8.45 pm, had been provided. Later the same year a request from Knaresborough town authorities for Sunday trains between Harrogate, Knaresborough and York, more excursions to and from Knaresborough and through carriages to Leeds was refused. Knaresborough station was extended in 1892 but the following year a passenger complained the first class gentlemen's waiting room had been marked "Ladies Room Third Class" and another room, for first class gentlemen passengers, had for some time been devoid of furniture, there not even being a chair to sit on.

At one time York trains used a station inside the city walls but in 1877 the present York station opened. In 1874 a man called McKenzie, called on Mr Bass, a Harrogate brickmaker. He said he was an agent for the contractor building the station and wished to place an order for 30,000 bricks. Delighted with such a large order Bass treated him to dinner after which McKenzie said he must dash if he was to catch the train to York. On searching his pockets

On 3rd March 1972 Class 31 diesel loco No. 5521 ran away from Harrogate goods yard and smashed through the level crossing gates at Starbeck, miraculously without hitting any vehicles on the busy main road. Signalmen down the line were informed and kept their gates open for it. Control suggested to the Marston Moor signalman if the unmanned loco had slowed down when it reached him he might jump aboard and stop it, and this he did. Later alterations to the goods yard meant trains could only enter and leave it near Harrogate North signal box and not at Dragon.

About 20 passengers were taken to hospital when the 7.33 am Leeds - Harrogate - York rammed the buffers at York station on the 6th February 1986. In another incident, on 24th November 1990, a Harrogate bound train ran into a car that had been driven onto the level crossing at Millfield Lane, Poppleton. The crossing had been converted to an automatic crossing in November 1986.

Plate 7.7   Poppleton station still retains its platform canopy to this day. On 19th March 1960 a Metro Cammell DMU calls with the 2.15pm Harrogate – York working. The stations at Allerton (later renamed Hopperton), Cattal and Marston Moor were all built to the same style but have lost their canopies in recent years. The siding in the foreground leads over the road, equipped with its own set of gates, to coal cells situated behind the down platform.   D.J. Williamson collection.

HESSAY

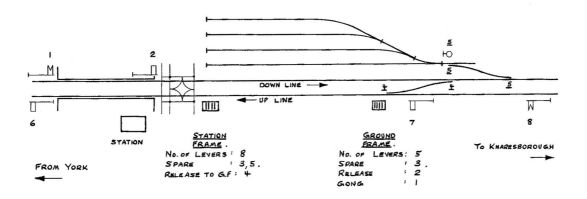

Plate 8.1   When first opened Ripley Valley station was called Killinghall but was quickly renamed Ripley one month after the branch opened in May 1862 and was renamed again to Ripley Valley in April 1875. Goods facilities were not provided at first but were later installed in 1881. D.J. Williamson collection.

Plate 8.2   Darley station was opened in 1864 two years after the branch was completed. The headshunt line on the right served two goods sidings behind the station building. Goods facilities were withdrawn in October 1953.   D.J. Williamson collection.

Chapter 8

THE PATELEY BRIDGE
BRANCH

The L & T had proposed a branch from Starbeck to Prospect Place, Harrogate, but on 22nd July 1848 they obtained an Act which gave them permission to abandon the upper part of this branch and build instead a branch from Starbeck to Pateley Bridge. Later lack of money, and a growing belief that such branches would be unprofitable, led the L & T to abandon the idea. Work had actually started on this branch when a cutting north of Starbeck had been dug to obtain soil to help form an embankment on the Pannal contract. On 18th May 1848 no less than 430 men removed 1,239 tons of soil from this cutting.

After the opening of the line between Leeds and Thirsk a twice-daily omnibus service had been started between Pateley Bridge and Nidd Bridge station, but what Nidderdale folk wanted was a railway to Pateley Bridge. Eventually, after agreeing to raise half the capital and sell the land needed at an agricultural price, they persuaded the NER to build one. The Act authorising the line was obtained on 21st July 1859. When this became known in Pateley Bridge the peace of the town was shattered by mortars being fired and a band marching the streets until late. On 20th September 1860 a procession left Ripley Castle and proceeded through Ripley, which was decorated with flags, towards Killinghall. On nearing the bridge over the Nidd it entered a field through a floral archway, which bore the motto, in chrysanthemums, "Success to the Nidd Valley Railway". Here the first sod was turned by the Rev H J Inglby of Ripley Castle. The line, which was single track, differed from the earlier proposal in that it left the L & T main line at Ripley Jct., south of Nidd Bridge, and not at Starbeck. It opened on 1st May 1862, although the collapse of the Bower Road bridge in Harrogate, two days earlier, meant trains could not use Harrogate station and probably used Starbeck. On the opening day huge crowds greeted the flower bedecked train at each station, and at Pateley Bridge a local manufacturer, George Metcalfe, the leading figure in bringing the railway to the dale, was carried around in a chair while a band played "See the Conquering Hero Comes." Unfortunately the NER directors and officials could not be present as they were in London attending the International Exhibition. Later that afternoon at a lunch at the George Hotel, Pateley Bridge, Metcalfe said although he was not a literary man whenever he had had doubts as to whether the branch would be built he had been encouraged by the words of Shakespeare. "Our doubts are traitors and would make us lose the good we might oft win by failing to attempt."

The first timetable showed four trains in each direction on weekdays and no Sunday service. The average journey time for the $14\frac{1}{2}$ miles between Harrogate and Pateley Bridge was 40 minutes. At first the only intermediate stations were Killinghall, Birstwith and Dacre, but Darley was added in 1864, and Hampsthwaite in 1866. Killinghall was later renamed Ripley Valley. There were no goods facilities at Ripley Valley until at least 1881 for that year the NER were asked to provide them. At Hampsthwaite goods facilities were never provided.

Railway staff at Dacre became suspicious in 1867, coal in the station yard appeared to be disappearing. P C Farrar was put on watch and at 3.30 am caught a Dacre man, William Bray, leaving the yard carrying a sack of coal on his back. Bray pleaded guilty and was sent to prison for 14 days. A retired surgeon on alighting from a train at Birstwith in 1867 decided to walk down the line towards his home because rain had made the road muddy and filled potholes with water. He was only a few yards from the place where he would have stepped from the railway onto his own property when he was struck by a train. His gravestone record that, "Without a word of warning he was called from this world by the fatal blow of an engine while walking on the Nidd Valley Railway".

During an enginemen's strike in 1867 the 3.15 pm from Pateley Bridge ran into the rear of a goods train at Dacre. A rumour spread that, because of amateurs employed as enginemen, a serious accident had occurred. This was denied by the NER who stated the driver had 15 years experience, and had been unable to stop because rain had made the rails slippery. Only two passengers, and a guard, had been slightly injured.

On the Pateley Bridge branch in November 1879 there were still only four trains in each direction on weekdays.

These ran as follows:

	AM	AM	PM	PM	PM
Harrogate dep.		8.55	12.05	4.35	7.30
Pateley Bridge arr.		9.43	12.43	5.12	8.07
Pateley Bridge dep.	7.35	10.25	3.00	5.55	
Harrogate arr.	8.10	11.00	3.35	6.30	

The 8.55 am from Harrogate ran first to Nidd Bridge before returning to Ripley Jct. and .proceeding to Pateley Bridge.

In 1878 the Postmaster General had offered £100 towards the cost of a train to reach Pateley Bridge before 8.00 am, but this had been refused. A request made in April 1887 for a train to enable summer visitors to leave Pateley Bridge later than 5.55 pm, the time the last train left for Harrogate, was also refused. However a request for a roof over the station platform at Pateley Bridge was granted. Prior to this there was no cover on the platform and little room in the waiting rooms.

Two men engaged in quarrying stone for Hull docks at the Wilson Wood quarry were struck by a train at Birstwith one evening in December 1881. They were returning to Harrogate and seeing the train approaching ran across the line to reach Birstwith station more quickly than if they used the public road. One of the men later died and a verdict of accidentally killed while trespassing on the NER was returned.

Extensive flooding occurred in the Nidd Valley in 1892. Had it not been for the bywash arches at Killinghall bridge damage to the railway would have been considerable. Ripley Valley station became an island and an immense quantity of ballast was washed from the line. During the night the flooded river rushed through Pateley Bridge station, but serious damage was prevented by the stationmaster calling out his men and having them erect a flood barrier. The small Scot Gate Ash tramway, which served a local quarry, was however severely damaged. The next day mail had to be taken from Pateley Bridge Post Office to the railway station by raft and the first train took over three hours to reach Harrogate owing to the line between Darley and Ripley being underwater.

In December 1866 a Pateley Bridge stonemason was fined £1 8s 6d for a breach of the NER by-laws. He had run a great risk of an accident by attempting to get into a train whilst it was in motion at Dacre station but had been prevented from doing so by Mr Hurst the stationmaster. One Saturday evening in July 1902 two young ladies attempted to board the 7.40 pm Pateley Bridge - Harrogate train as it was moving off from Birstwith station. Mr Forster, the stationmaster, shouted a warning but they persisted and in their hurry one fell between the platform and the moving train. She was saved from serious injury by the stationmaster holding her and preventing her from falling further down. She was dragged about 12 yards before the train could be stopped but suffered no more than embarrassment as her dress skirt was torn off.

In the late 1870s the loco which worked the last train of the day to Pateley Bridge is said to have had a unique loud whistle which would be sounded five minutes before the train was due to depart. This served as a warning to Nidderdale folk still in Harrogate's public houses to drink up and board the train. In summer 1923 a petrol-electric railcar, stabled at Starbeck, worked on the branch but, despite being described by the Harrogate station master as a step in the right direction, left the area that autumn. In later years "Push-pull" units with Class G5, 0-4-4T, locos provided the passenger service. The loco was kept in a timber built engine shed at Pateley Bridge where a 42 ft 6 in turntable was also provided.

After the First World War the railways began to face increasing competition from road transport. During a rail strike in 1924 Pateley Bridge trains ran as normal but Nidderdale dairymen had ready, if needed, a motor service which, it was claimed, could deliver milk to the Leeds depots with little or no delay.

During the last weekend of February 1933 over 100,000 tons of snow fell on Harrogate. Buses came to a standstill but few trains were stopped, despite drifts four or five feet deep. On 25th February the last train to Pateley Bridge had to be dug out of deep drifts and took over three hours to complete a journey normally done in half an hour. The line was also blocked by fallen telegraph poles and in the morning the first train from Pateley Bridge was unable to get through.

Plate 8.3   All the intermediate stations on the branch had single platforms. As there was only one scheduled passenger working on the branch at any one time this was not an operational hindrance considering the daily goods train could be shunted into one of the station goods yards when the passenger train was due. Here we see Dacre around the turn of the century.   Robert Scott/NERA Library.

Plate 8.4   The stone built engine shed at Pateley Bridge was replaced at an unknown date by a wooden structure shown here. One theory suggests that the weight of the stone structure built on the edge of the River Nidd was too much, leading to its replacement. Pateley Bridge signal box, latterly equipped with a frame of 29 levers, stands opposite with a water tank behind to feed the engine shed water column. Once passenger services ended in 1951 the branch was worked under 'one engine in steam' regulations.   Ken Hoole collection

BIRSTWITH

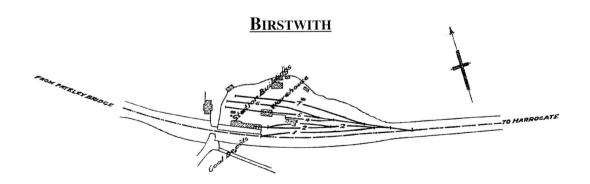

The number of trains on the branch changed little over the years. In December 1933 trains ran as follows:

Mondays to Fridays

	AM	AM	PM	PM
Pateley Bridge dep.	7.30	10.05	1.28	5.25
Harrogate arr.	8.05	10.39	2.01	6.03

On Saturdays additional trains ran as follows,

	AM	PM	PM
Pateley Bridge dep.	11.45	3.45	8.08
Harrogate arr.	12.18	4.22	8.39

In the opposite direction trains, Mondays to Fridays were,

	AM	PM	PM	PM
Harrogate dep.	9.10	12.25	4.35	6.26
Pateley Bridge arr.	9.45	12.59	5.09	6.59

On Saturdays additional trains were,

	AM	PM	PM
Harrogate dep.	10.58	2.27	9.25
Pateley Bridge arr.	11.32	3.01	9.57

On Sundays there was one train in each direction,

	AM
Harrogate dep.	8.20
Pateley Bridge arr.	8.54
Pateley Bridge dep.	9.12
Harrogate arr.	9.52

In Summer 1939 through trains between Leeds and Pateley Bridge ran on Sundays, but after the Second World War the branch began to decline. Hampsthwaite station closed to passengers on 2nd January 1950 and from 25th September the timetable showed, Mondays to Fridays,

	AM	PM
Pateley Bridge dep.	8.13	1.17
Harrogate arr.	8.45	1.49
Harrogate dep.	9.03	5.35
Pateley Bridge arr.	9.35	6.05

And on Saturdays,

	AM	AM	PM	PM
Pateley Bridge dep.	8.13	9.46		2.15
Harrogate arr.	8.45	10.18		2.47
Harrogate dep.	9.03		1.25	5.35
Pateley Bridge arr.	9.35		1.57	6.05

The 5.35 pm from Harrogate did not call at Ripley Valley otherwise all intermediate stations were served. There was no Sunday service. The stationmaster at Ripley Valley from 1938 to his retirement in 1953 was Mr A Wade. One of his many recollections was of lending his walking stick to King George VI when the King spent the night in the Royal Train at Ripley Valley during the war.

In 1950 British Railways announced the five remaining stations on the branch issued, on average, only five tickets a day each and unless traffic improved the passenger service would be

Plate 8.5   A postcard, dated 1908, shows the scene at Pateley Bridge after the arrival of a lengthy train, probably a market day or excursion train. Engine No. 832, a 0-6-0 of class 398 designed by Fletcher and completed in September 1873, stands at the head of about ten coaches. The stone built station building has stepped gables of the 1860's period, a style also used at other stations on the branch such as Birstwith, Dacre and Ripley Valley but also elsewhere, Goathland, Danby and Lealholm being examples. In the background on the right can be seen the original engine shed building with the same stepped gable ends.   Lens of Sutton/ Ken Hoole collection.

Plate 8.6   For many years Pateley Bridge engine shed stabled an ex-NER class O (later LNER class G5) 0-4-4T for the passenger service to Harrogate. In LNER days the resident member of this class was No. 1839 (later BR No. 67253) but here Starbeck based No. 67284 (NER/LNER No. 1886) is in charge of the single coach train on 8th April 1950. The coach is an NER toplight pattern brake composite to diagram 162 built in 1908. Both locomotive and coach are fitted for push-pull working.   Ken Hoole collection.

withdrawn. This brought accusations that trains times were deliberately inconvenient and fares were higher than those on competing buses in an effort to deter passengers and justify withdrawal of the passenger service. Despite protests the last regular passenger train, hauled by Class G5, 0-4-4T, No. 67253, ran on 31st March 1951 - Local MPs protested and asked train services be restored using a more economical diesel railcar but the BTC replied a diesel railcar would not make the Nidd Valley branch profitable. They believed a railcar would be unable to compete with buses, and it was not government policy for the BTC to compete with itself by attracting passengers to trains at the expense of buses. A further request for the restoration of the passenger service using BR diesel multiple units was made by Pateley Bridge Rural District Council in 1955, following the introduction of such units in the Harrogate area, but this request was also refused.

Goods traffic continued on the branch until 31st October 1964 when the branch closed completely. Apart from demolition trains the last loco to work the branch was Class J27, 0-6-0, No. 65894. Darley had closed to goods on 1st October 1953 and Ripley Valley on 6th November 1961. On 19th October 1963 LMS Class 4P, 2-6-4T, No. 42409 had worked an enthusiast's special to Pateley Bridge and on 12th March 1964 a local school hired a DMU to give school children their first, and last, trip on the branch.

DARLEY

BILTON JUNCTION

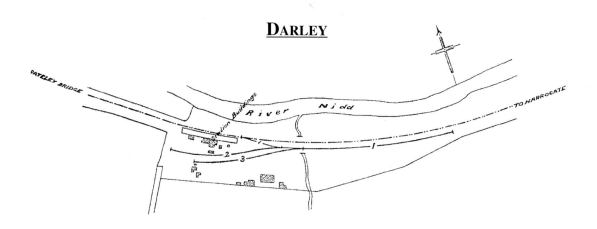

NO. OF LEVERS : 40 , No.1 : GATEWHEEL.
SPARE : 9,38.

REFERENCES : NER ENGINEERS OFFICE, YORK,
DRG. No. SI4/27E/9, DATED 17·6·1913.
PRO MT6/2229/1.
DRAWN : 23/11/88

Chapter 9

THE HARROGATE GAS WORKS RAILWAY

After the opening of the railway at Starbeck coal was transported from there to the gas works at New Park by road. In 1852 a request from local residents for a coal and lime siding at Bilton and, although there was no station at Bilton, for a return train to Knaresborough on market days was refused. In 1880 increased coal consumption at the gas works led to a siding being laid at Bilton Jct. From here coal was carried to the gas works, 1½ miles away, in trailers hauled by traction engines. Unfortunately these damaged the roads and in 1897 the gas company asked the NER, unsuccessfully, for a line from Bilton Jct. to the gas works. They were no more successful in 1902 when Harrogate Corporation joined in on the request. The gas company, therefore, built their own 2 ft gauge line from Bilton Jct. to the gas works. The first sod was ceremoniously turned on 7th May 1907, although work on a tunnel under Skipton Road had started on 25th April. By November 1908 the line was fully open.

The first loco to work trains on the railway was a 0-6-2ST built by T Green & Sons of Leeds in 1908 and named "Barber" after the Chairman of the gas company. In 1920 another loco, an ex War Department 4-6-0T, built the previous year, was bought, modified and named "Spencer" after the Vice-Chairman. "Spencer" was not a success, even after the line was deviated slightly to reduce a gradient the loco found difficult to climb with a train. "Barber" continued to do most of the work but in 1944 a new loco, a Peckett 0-6-0ST, was bought. Five years later another new loco, a 0-6-0 Drewry diesel, arrived. Rolling stock consisted of six steel hopper wagons and two tank wagons for carrying tar and ammoniacal liquor.

The line, which was single track with a passing loop, ran mainly through open country and was unfenced, but cattle guards existed where necessary. At Bilton railway owned hopper wagons discharged coal through their bottom doors into holding hoppers. From here chutes fed the narrow gauge gas works wagons on a lower level. For the loading of the tar and liquor the situation was reversed with BR wagons being loaded from the gas works wagons standing on a dock at a higher level. The line closed completely in October 1956 after road transport proved more economical. The diesel loco was sold for use elsewhere but "Barber" was secured for preservation and left for Leeds on 10th April 1957. The Peckett has also been preserved but "Spencer" was scrapped in 1946.

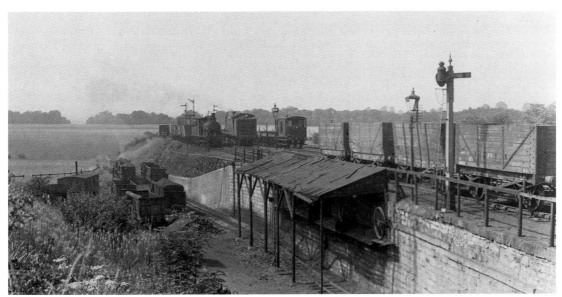

Plate 9.1   A view of the Harrogate Gas Works exchange sidings on 9th July 1949 showing hopper and bottom door standard gauge coal wagons standing above the covered discharge chutes. In the narrow gauge sidings Peckett 0-6-0ST, works no. 2049, built in 1944, shunts loaded narrow gauge bogie hopper wagons. To the north above the narrow gauge complex class J21 0-6-0, No.65041 and class A6 4-6-2T, No. 9793 stand in Bilton Sidings awaiting banking duties.   C.H.A. Townley/J.A.Peden collection

Plate 10.1 The Station at Pateley Bridge with a train of ex Metropolitan coaches bought by the NVLR. On the left, adjacent to wooden goods shed, stands one of the open wagons built by Hurst Nelson for Bradford Corporation (note the lettering). Also note the moveable cattle hurdle used for loading wagons with livestock.   Ken Hoole collection.

Plate 10.2   Railcar 'Hill' had originally been built for the Great Western Railway by Kerr Stewart in 1905. It was sold by the GWR in 1920 to the dealer, J.F. Wake of Darlington, who later resold the railcar to Bradford Corporation with whom it entered service in July 1920. It was named after Sir James Hill, one time Lord Mayor of Bradford. 'Hill' is pictured at Pateley Bridge in front of the signal box, other stations had a lever frame on the platform.   RAS Marketing.

Plate 10.3   'Milner' stands at Lofthouse station during 1928. This engine was built in 1909 by Hudswell Clarke & Co., Leeds, at a cost of £1,300. It handled many of the passenger services on the line. After closure of the line it was sold at auction in 1937 to Sir Lindsay Parkinson, the contractor 'Milner' was last noted at a South Wales opencast coal mine in 1956.   RAS Marketing.

Chapter 10

THE NIDD VALLEY LIGHT RAILWAY

In 1901 a line was proposed from Pateley Bridge to Lofthouse by a company known as Power and Traction Ltd. Unfortunately they were unable to raise sufficient capital but the scheme was taken over by Bradford Corporation, who were building reservoirs in upper Nidderdale. Work on building the line began in July 1904. The following year the Pateley Bridge engine shed of John Best & Sons Ltd., the contractor building the line, was destroyed by fire and a loco inside was severely damaged. Despite this the line opened in September 1907. A passenger service was provided between Pateley Bridge and Lofthouse, a distance of approximately 6 miles. A further 6½ miles to Angram was used mainly to carry workmen and materials to the reservoirs. On 29th November 1911 a Lofthouse - Pateley Bridge passenger train ran into a rail placed across the line south of Ramsgill. A stone had also been placed inside a check rail by, it was thought, a workman dismissed from the reservoirs, but no derailment occurred.

The NVLR was of standard gauge and was connected to the NER at Pateley Bridge, where both companies had their own station, but there was never a regular through passenger service. Passengers had to alight and walk between the two stations. In October 1920 trains ran as follows,

	AM	AM	PM	PM	PM
Harrogate dep.		9.15	12.25	4.00	6.23
Pateley Bridge NER arr.		9.54	1.08	4.37	7.01
Pateley Bridge NVLR dep.	8.30	10.25	1.30	5.00	
Lofthouse arr.	8.55	10.50	1.55	5.25	

	AM	AM	AM	PM	PM
Lofthouse dep.		9.10	11.05	3.15	5.40
Pateley Bridge NVLR arr.		9.30	11.25	3.35	6.00
Pateley Bridge NER dep.	7.25	10.10	1.25	4.50	
Harrogate arr.	8.06	10.50	2.01	5.28	

On Saturdays an extra train left Pateley Bridge for Harrogate at 8.00 pm and arrived back in Pateley Bridge at 9.58 pm

Locomotives used to work the passenger trains initially consisted of two ex-Metropolitan Railway 4-4-0Ts, "Holdsworth" and "Milner". A Hudswell Clarke 0-6-0T, replaced the previous "Milner" in 1909. An 0-4-0T, named "Gadie", was also bought from Hudswell Clarke in 1920. The most unusual addition from July 1920 was an ex-Great Western Railway steam railcar, which the NVLR named "Hill". The carriages used for the public passenger service between Pateley Bridge and Lofthouse had previously seen service on the Metropolitan.

John Best & Sons were also the contractors for the building of both the Angram and Scar House Reservoirs, using their own locomotives on goods trains from Pateley Bridge and on work around the construction sites. At least 10 different locos were used at various times. From the mid-1920s the contractor also had ex-Maryport & Carlisle Railway coaches to transport workmen to the construction sites.

Competition from buses led to the withdrawal of the passenger service on 31st December 1929 but the line remained in use until the completion of Scar House Reservoir in 1936. Four months after the withdrawal of the passenger service Pateley Bridge Rural District Council complained there were about 56 buses running in Nidderdale and the roads were suffering. At least one councillor believed there were too many buses and an unnecessary amount of transport to Lofthouse.

Plate 11.1 A NER Fletcher design 0-6-0, No. 783, built by Robert Stephenson & Co. in 1872 stands on the carriage sidings turntable at Bradford Foster Square station between turns from Harrogate. Classified by Thomas Worsdell as class 398 the engine is seen in NER post-1904 lined black livery. It was withdrawn in 1911. The North Eastern and LNER stationed an engine at the Midland Railway shed at Manningham for many years. LGRP/D.J. Williamson collection.

Plate 11.2 An overall view of Otley station looking east after the arrival of a Harrogate – Bradford service in NER days. The train is comprised of a mixture of NER clerestory and elliptical stock, a solitary Midland Railway clerestory coach stands in the right hand siding. D.J. Williamson collection.

Chapter 11

HARROGATE - OTLEY - BRADFORD

On 1st February 1865 a line was opened between Arthington and Otley, and on 1st August the same year was extended to Ilkley. On 1st August 1877 the NER began running through trains between Harrogate and Bradford using this line and the Midland Railway's newly opened Guiseley - Shipley line. At first there were three trains in each direction per weekday but by 1879 the number had increased to four. Despite the increase there were complaints that the first trains, the 8.40 am from Harrogate and the 10.25 am from Bradford, left too late for businessmen and the last, the 7.00 pm from Harrogate and the 8.20 pm from Bradford, left too early for theatre-goers. By 1887 the number had increased to six in each direction, with Otley and Shipley the only intermediate stops. The first train from Harrogate, at 8.45 am, still left too late for businessmen but the first from Bradford now left at 7.35 am and arrived in Harrogate at 8.22 am. The last train from Harrogate to Bradford left at 7.35 pm, whilst the last train left Bradford at 8.45 pm. By 1900 the number of trains had increased to nine in each direction. All but one also stopped at Guiseley and some stopped at Pannal on alternate Mondays for passengers attending the livestock sales. Some also stopped at Weeton on request. The first trains were now the 7.38 am from Harrogate and the 7.28 am from Bradford. The last were the 7.46 pm from Harrogate and the 8.50 pm from Bradford.

In 1923 most British Railway companies were compelled by Parliament to amalgamate into four large companies. The NER was amongst those, which formed the LNER, but the Midland Railway was amongst those, which formed the LMS. This meant that there were still two companies involved in running the Harrogate - Otley - Bradford Forster Square service. This service, and that between Harrogate and Leeds, was well used by commuters and some trains carried Club Saloons, which were more like gentlemen's clubs than railway carriages.

The NER had improved the Harrogate - Bradford Forster Square service in 1919 after complaints about the slow and unpunctual trains. The complaints, however, continued, culminating in 1926 when Bradford businessmen threatened to boycott the LNER and divert wool carrying ships from east to west coast ports unless services, including those between Harrogate and Bradford, were improved. The LNER replied it could not improve the Bradford Forster Square service without the co-operation of the LMS, and it was difficult to improve the speed of trains because weight restrictions on the Milner Wood bridge, near Otley, meant more powerful locos could not be used.

In May 1939 there were, Mondays to Fridays, seven trains in each direction between Harrogate and Bradford Forster Square. On Saturdays there was an extra train in each direction, but no Sunday service. The first train from Bradford, at 8.55 am, was a through train to Newcastle, via Ripon and Thirsk. Ten years later, in May 1949, there were only two trains in each direction between Harrogate and Bradford Forster Square, Mondays to Fridays. These left Harrogate at 8.25 am and 3.25 pm and arrived in Bradford at 9.18 am and 4.17 pm. In the opposite direction trains left Bradford at 10.35 am and 5.15 pm and arrived in Harrogate at 11.20 am and 6.06 pm. On Saturdays there was only one train in each direction, the 8.25 am from Harrogate, and one at 12.23 pm from Bradford, which arrived in Harrogate at 1.14 pm. In February 1957 the only trains were the 8.25 am from Harrogate, which arrived in Bradford at 9.19 am, and the 5.15 pm from Bradford which arrived in Harrogate at 6.12 pm. On Saturdays the departure time from Bradford was 12.23 pm, with arrival in Harrogate at 1.14 pm. The Harrogate - Bradford Forster Square service was withdrawn from 25th February 1957 but in summer 1960 congestion at Leeds resulted in 11 diesel trains in each direction being run, on Sundays only, between Bradford Forster Square and Knaresborough, via Otley.

Passenger services were withdrawn from Arthington, Pool in Wharfedale and Otley from 22nd March 1965 and from 5th July 1965 the line between Arthington and Burley Jct., where the Leeds - Ilkley line was joined, closed completely. At various times in NER days there had been a through service between Harrogate and Bolton Abbey and between Harrogate and Skipton. In later years the line had been used by trains between the North - East and Lancashire. On summer Saturdays in 1952 there had been a Saltburn - Blackpool service, which called at Otley. In 1953 a through York - Harrogate - Skipton service had run on summer Saturdays. Goods trains had included Newport - Heysham Moss tanker trains, which ran via Ripon and Skipton. In September 1963 there had been one such train in each direction per weekday.

Plate 12.1   *The station master and his sons stand for the camera in the early 1900s at Copgrove station. Note the display of plants in the gardens and the signal box on the Knaresborough end of the platform.   K.L. Taylor collection.*

Plate 12.2   *During the General Strike of 1926 the LNER borrowed the Derwent Valley Light Railway's twin Ford railbus for use on the branch. The railbus pair is seen at Knaresborough with station staff. When the DVLR ceased passenger services in August 1926 the railbuses were sold to the County Donegal Railway in Ireland.   Ken Hoole collection*

Chapter 12

THE BOROUGHBRIDGE BRANCH

On 17th June 1847 the Great North of England Railway opened a line from Pilmoor to Boroughbridge. The "Harrogate Advertiser" however was not impressed for it reported 'Thursday last was a memorable day in the history of Boroughbridge, the Railway King having for the first time sent his snorting steeds over the iron pathway to inspire the inhabitants of that decayed little town with an idea they were now reposed on a bed of roses and dreaming of prosperity to be henceforth realised'. In other words the Boroughbridge and Pilmoor branch was opened for the accommodation of the public. There was no unmeaning ceremony and only three small flags floated in the air. Two were inscribed "Hudson" and Lawson". The third was a Union Jack. There was also a forest of pocket handkerchiefs and a white banner bearing the inscription, in plain characters, 'Town and Trade of Boroughbridge'. A little before noon four engines, and a number of carriages occupied by a fair sprinkling of the surrounding gentry and a few of the directors, approached the station amid the discordant clang of drums, brass instruments and the deafening shouts of the populous, hundreds of whom had arrived to witness the first arrival of all potent steam. One or two of the engines were decorated with evergreens and flowers and for a moment, at the first arrival, the effort was rather imposing but its fine appearance quickly vanished as the multitude dispersed. There was no public luncheon at this stage of the proceedings, nor was there anything of this kind so as long as we remained in the town, but it was expected the directors, contractors and others would subsequently partake of an entertainment at the Greyhound Hotel.

It was proposed, by the YNMR, to link the Pilmoor - Boroughbridge branch to the Harrogate - Church Fenton line, then under construction, by a line through Knaresborough. The L & T opposed this by promoting their own Knaresborough - Boroughbridge branch but Parliament favoured the YNMR, apparently because the L & T branch would have had no connection with the Pilmoor branch at Boroughbridge. Later financial circumstances meant the YNMR never built their Boroughbridge branch. If they had they would have had to share the viaduct at Knaresborough with the L & Ts Starbeck - Knaresborough branch.

In 1864 Knaresborough and Boroughbridge people unsuccessfully petitioned the NER for a line between the two places. The following year a new company, the Leeds North Yorkshire & Durham Railway, proposed a line from Leeds to Stockton, via Wetherby and Easingwold. Also proposed were a number of branches, including one to Scarborough. To counter this the NER obtained powers, on 23rd June 1866, for lines from Cross Gates to Wetherby, and from Knaresborough to Boroughbridge, which with existing lines and new loops would form a new route to Scarborough. The LNY & D proposal was rejected by Parliament, because the costs of construction had been underestimated, and soon after the NER bought out the leading promoters. With the would be competitor gone the NER sought powers to abandon its Wetherby and Boroughbridge schemes but were opposed by Leeds, Wetherby and Boroughbridge. The NER therefore agreed to build their Wetherby and Boroughbridge lines but obtained powers in August 1869 allowing them extra time to do so.

The Knaresborough - Boroughbridge line was staked out in July 1870 but tenders to build it were not sought until November 1871. During construction on 14th October 1873 one navvy was killed, and two seriously injured, when 17 ballast wagons ran away and were derailed, and in winter 1874/5 severe weather stopped all work for ten weeks.

At Boroughbridge the line crossed the Ure by a bridge, the piers of which had to be sunk 40 feet below the river bed to gain a solid foundation. Because the line had to gain height to cross the river it was too high to make an end to end connection with the branch from Pilmoor. This branch was therefore joined two furlongs from its former Boroughbridge terminus. This meant a new Boroughbridge station had to be provided because the old one was bypassed. The old station however remained in use for goods traffic. The NER promised the line, which was single track, would be open by 23rd July 1874 but it was no until 1st April 1875 that the line was, unceremoniously, opened. The first service consisted of five trains in each direction between Harrogate and Pilmoor each weekday.

The tender of a locomotive starting a passenger train out of Boroughbridge on 8 November 1869 became derailed on points, broke away from the loco and turned across the line. Fortunately the train had not gathered sufficient speed for the accident to be serious.

On 8th November 1876 three horses belonging to Treblesyke Farm strayed on to the line near Brafferton and were struck by a Pilmoor bound train. Two empty carriages were derailed and narrowly avoided falling into the Swale. What passengers there were continued to Pilmoor on the loco.

In 1879, following a request from Boroughbridge residents, the NER agreed to deliver goods free of charge in Boroughbridge.

The body of the foreman platelayer of the Boroughbridge - Brafferton section of line was found in the Swale in 1888. He had fallen asleep by the railway bridge after drinking five glasses of whisky and it was assumed fallen into the river when aroused by the passing of the 6.00 pm train. The coroner's jury recommended the company's attention be drawn to their workmen spending time in public houses.

In the early hours of one December morning in 1904 Boroughbridge station caught fire. The railway staff were called out but the only fire-fighting appliance was a hand pump from the Boroughbridge Brewery. Consequently the booking office was destroyed, the porter's room burnt out and the glass veranda over the platform damaged.

Occasionally diverted trains ran over the line. This was so on 12th February 1930 when the down West Riding Pullman was diverted via Starbeck and Boroughbridge after it arrived at Harrogate to find its route north blocked by a derailed loco at Ripon.

After a severe snowstorm at the end of February 1933 40 telegraph poles, snapped by the weight of snow, blocked the branch.

In the 1930s the Depression and competition from road transport forced the LNER to seek economies. The passenger service on the Boroughbridge branch was considered for withdrawal but instead a signalling system was introduced which it was hoped would reduce the cost of working the branch. Ordinary semaphore signals were superseded by various fixed and movable boards. Station distant signals were replaced by location marker boards painted with black and white diagonal stripes and white reflex lenses in zigzag form. These location marker boards were located 900 yards from stations. Section limit boards, painted with red and white diagonal stripes, and studded with a border of white reflex lenses, with three clusters of red lenses down the centre, replaced home signals between 150 and 200 yards from stations. At stations station boards, painted white, and able to rotate on a vertical axis to face up or down trains, could exhibit in the centre a green square in daylight and a green light at night. This would permit trains to pass a section limit board and proceed as far as the station only. A train could only restart from a station after the person in charge had received permission from the signalbox ahead, and the driver had the correct staff or ticket. Gate caution boards, 600 yards from level crossings, acted as gate distant signals and were interlocked with the gates. Painted with two yellow and two black diamonds, which formed one large diamond on a white background, and studded with white reflex lenses spelling GATE, they worked on an horizontal axis and in the clear position the face of the board was not visible. Corresponding to gate stop signals were gate stop boards. These had a red diamond painted on a white background with white reflex lenses arranged vertically spelling STOP. At Pilmoor and Wath Lane, where the gates opened away from the railway, the board was interlocked with the gates and worked on a horizontal axis. When in the clear position the face of the board was not visible. At the two other crossings, Humberton and Myton Lane, the gates closed across the railway and the boards were fixed to the gates.

The lenses on all the boards were illuminated at night by a powerful headlamp carried on whilst the left side of the locomotive's bufferbeam. This was fitted at Harrogate but only switched on whilst on the branch. The usual headcode was also carried. In an emergency spares for the headlamp could be obtained from Knaresborough and Pilmoor. Spare headlamps were also kept at Pilmoor for use of special and excursion trains coming onto the branch from that direction. Because of the difficulty in obtaining the correct type of accumulator to power the headlamp the introduction of the system was delayed for some months.

The first train to use the headlamp was the 4.45 pm Harrogate - Pilmoor on 12th February 1936. After the outbreak of war the headlamp ceased to be used. From 8th September 1939 new regulations stated before a train was allowed to leave a staff station in rear of the level crossings the signalman, or person in charge, had to obtain an assurance by telephone from the crossing keeper that the gates were across the road. The crossing keeper had then to exhibit a green light,

Plate 12.3 The first station at Boroughbridge built by the Great North of England Railway served its purpose until 1875. When the line was extended to Knaresborough it diverged before the terminus and ran through a new station and over a bridge crossing the River Ure. In this view the original locomotive shed can be seen on the left (converted into a goods warehouse), with the main goods shed and old station buildings beyond. Ken Hoole collection.

Plate 12.4 The new station had two platforms either side of a passing loop, the single story buildings being on the south side. By the end of 19th century the Pilmoor bound platform had fallen out of use, thereafter sometimes being used as a loading dock. The signal box on the platform end held a fifteen lever frame. D.J. Williamson collection

if it was safe for the train to approach, or a red light if it was not. With the return of peace the headlamp was reinstated but after the withdrawal of the passenger service in 1950 this signalling system, unique to the Boroughbridge branch, was abandoned.

By 1950 the average number of passengers using the Boroughbridge branch was only 15 a day. Consequently the passenger service was withdrawn from 25th September 1950. In latter years Push-pull trains worked by Class G5 locos had provided the service. The last regular passenger train was worked by Class G5, 0-4-4T, No. 67337. Interestingly in 1926, during the General Strike, a twin Ford railbus, borrowed from the Derwent Valley Light Railway at York, had been used on the branch.

In November 1879 the timetable was:

	AM	AM	PM	PM
Pilmoor dep.	8.22	10.38	1.37	5.40
Harrogate arr.	9.10	11.26	2.25	6.25
Harrogate dep.	9.30	11.55	4.25	7.25
Pilmoor arr.	10.17	12.40	5.12	8.12

There was also a train starting from Boroughbridge at 7.51 am and arriving at Pilmoor at 8.07 am and one from Pilmoor at 8.35 pm terminating at Boroughbridge at 8.51 pm.

In December 1933, Mondays to Fridays, there were only two trains in each direction each day.

	AM	PM
Harrogate dep.	6.50	4.45
Pilmoor arr.	7.26	5.21
Pilmoor dep.	8.08	5.52
Harrogate arr.	8.50	6.32

On Saturdays there were addition trains

	AM	AM	PM	PM
Harrogate dep.	6.50	11.50	4.45	7.45
Pilmoor arr.	7.26	12.26	5.21	8.21
Pilmoor dep.	8.08	1.30	5.52	8.53
Harrogate arr.	8.50	2.11	6.32	9.33

As usual there was no Sunday service.

COPGROVE

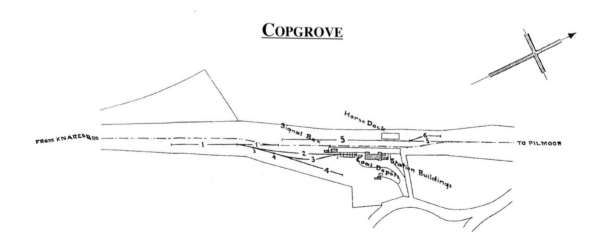

The final timetable issued in summer 1950, showed Mondays to Fridays:

	AM	PM
Harrogate dep.	6.40	5.00
Pilmoor arr.	7.18	5.40
Pilmoor dep.	8.06	6.16
Harrogate arr.	8.50	7.00

On Saturdays

	AM	PM	PM	PM	PM
Harrogate dep.	6.40	12.10	5.00	7.45	10.52
Pilmoor arr.	7.18	12.48	5.40	8.23	11.31.
Pilmoor dep.	8.06	1.28	6.16	8.48	
Harrogate arr.	8.50	2.10	7.00	9.30	

Trains were worked by a Starbeck loco, although in early years it is believed a shed at Boroughbridge provided the loco.

Shortly before the Second World War a rail connected Air Ministry depot was opened between Brafferton and Pilmoor. The section between the entrance to this depot and Pilmoor was partially lifted in September 1953, and Copgrove became a public delivery siding in January 1955. The same year the pickup goods began deliveries of fresh water to houses alongside the railway in Hazelheads lane, Knaresborough, after a well, previously used, became polluted. On 25th April 1964 an enthusiast's special hauled by Class 5, 4-6-0, No. 44790 worked an enthusiast's special to Boroughbridge. The branch closed completely from 6th October 1964.

Plate 12.5   Class G5 0-4-4T, No. 67289 (NER No. 1911) runs into Pilmoor on the last day of service (25th September 1950) past one of the board signals erected in 1936, when ordinary semaphore signals were replaced by various fixed and movable boards. Moor Siding diverges to the left of the board signal. The siding initially ran to a brick and tile works but was later used by local farmers for the loading of agricultural produce and timber. J.W.Hague/J.Rogers collection.

Plate 13.1 Masham station with NER 2-4-0ST, No. 84, with a train of three oil lit four wheel coaches sometime in the 1880s. No. 84, a rebuild of YN&BR 2-4-0, stands in front of the combined station and station masters house. British Railways/G.Pierson collection.

Plate 13.2 The Masham branch train stands at Ripon's down platform awaiting departure in LNER days behind class G5 0-4-4T, No. 1911. The engine stabled at Masham in 1923 had been a class F8 2-4-2, No. 1599, but by 1929 this had changed to engine illustrated. The coaches form the 'Ripon and Masham set' comprised of a Brake Third and Brake Composite, both NER clerestories in this view. Note: the water column above the engines dome and the double ground signals in the foreground protecting the trailing points leading to the goods yard on the up side and the up to down line crossover. G.Pierson collection.

Chapter 13

THE MASHAM BRANCH

In the 1860s the East & West Yorkshire Union Railway proposed a line from Sedbergh to Melmerby, via Leyburn and Masham. This was opposed by the Midland Railway, and the NER, with the result a new company, the Hawes & Melmerby Railway was formed. An act authorising the building of the railway was obtained in 1865. Later financial worries led to the abandonment of the scheme but the NER were persuaded to build a branch from Melmerby to Masham after local people offered to help finance its construction, and sell the land needed at an agricultural price. The Act authorising construction was obtained on 13th July 1871 and the line, which was single track, opened on 9th June 1875. On the opening day Masham was decorated with flags and triumphal arches. A procession marched through the streets and in the evening a dinner was held in the market place. Although Masham had a market place it had no market. The railway enabled the first to be held, on 23rd June 1875.

The branch passenger trains usually terminated at, or started from, Ripon rather than Melmerby. In November 1879 the service was:

	AM	PM	PM
Masham dep.	8.00	1.20	7.15
Ripon arr.	8.30	1.50	7.45
Ripon dep.	9.25	3.45	8.15
Masham arr.	9.55	4.15	8.45

There was also an extra train from Masham on Thursdays (market day).

In October 1908 a goods train, over which the driver had lost control, ran through the goods yard at Masham, across the road to Ripon, and into the exchange sidings smashing several wagons.

The loco that worked the passenger service, in latter years Class G5, 0-4-4T, No. 1911, was stabled at Masham. A wooden engine shed and 42 ft turntable were provided. In 1920 a passed fireman was transferred there from Thirsk, much against his will, to act as a driver whenever a regular driver was absent. Six weeks after his arrival a regular driver failed to take up duty and Starbeck shed was asked to provide a replacement. This so annoyed the passed fireman he went on strike and sent for his union rep who succeeded in getting him transferred back to Thirsk.

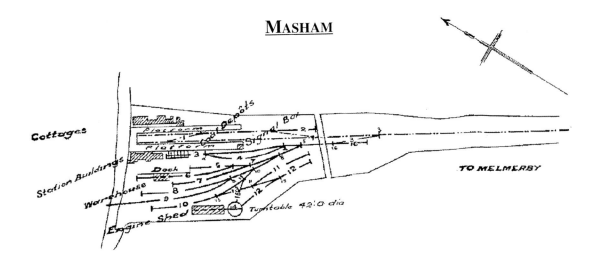

MASHAM

In October 1920 passenger trains ran as follows:

	AM	AM	PM	PM
Masham dep.	7.00	10.10	1.00	5.50
Ripon arr.	7.20	10.31	1.21	6.11
Ripon dep.	9.17	12.07	5.05	7.25
Masham arr.	9.39	12.46	5.27	7.47

There was no Sunday service.

In April 1926 the 12.20 pm passenger train to Masham was derailed between Tanfield and Masham but no one was seriously injured.

The passenger service was withdrawn from the Masham branch from 1st January 1931 although the branch continued to see the occasional excursion train. Goods traffic continued for another 32 years and during the Second World War an ammunition dump in the area created extra traffic. Officially the Masham branch closed completely from 11th November 1963 but coal traffic continued for a further week.

The building of Roundhill Reservoir by Harrogate Corporation led to a 2 ft gauge railway being built from Leighton to the dam in 1903. Two years later it was extended to exchange sidings opposite Masham goods yard. The line was later sold to Leeds Corporation who were building Leighton Reservoir. A train proceeding downhill near Leighton on the light railway on 29th May 1911 got out of control owing to the loco having insufficient braking power for the load carried. As the train rounded a curve at speed a load of timber fell off killing one man and seriously injuring another. After Leighton Reservoir was completed the line, which was approximately six miles long, fell into disuse and is thought to have been lifted around 1930.

Plate 13.3 *The building of a reservoir beyond Masham resulted in the building of a light railway and set of exchange sidings opposite Masham goods yard. On 8th October 1908 the Leeds driver of a Masham bound special goods hauled by NER McDonnell 0-6-0, No. 208, lost control of his train on the descent into the terminus. The result was that the train shot through the goods yard, crossed the main road on an extended siding serving the exchange sidings where it came to an abrupt halt with its train of wagons piled up behind it. Note the private owner coal wagon belonging to J & J. Charlesworth. Ken Hoole collection*

Chapter 14

STARBECK

At Starbeck there were two yards. Situated on the Knaresborough side of the level crossing was the marshalling yard, known officially as Stonefall sidings. Here too was the loco shed. On the Harrogate side of the crossing was the North Yard. This yard housed a tranship shed and coal depots. This yard was also a centre for the cleaning of cattle wagons and was equipped with a cattle dock which was used by a variety of livestock, including racing pigeons, which arrived for release in special trains. The Royal Canadian Mounted police, and cavalry regiments, also used the dock when they appeared at the Great Yorkshire Show.

In 1931 E.W. Bywell had been appointed coal agent at Starbeck. He had previously been the editor of the NER and LNER Magazines and was one of the founders, and first curator, of the original railway museum at York.

The level crossing at Starbeck, by which the railway crosses the main Harrogate-Knaresborough road, has been the subject of many complaints over the years. Almost every train movement at Starbeck involved using the crossing with consequent delays to road traffic. When the railway was under construction in 1847 some Harrogatonians asked for a bridge to be provided, others favoured a level crossing. They argued the closing of the gates would warn horsemen a train was approaching and give them time to ensure the horse was not frightened, but if a horseman was passing over a bridge, and a train suddenly dashed underneath, the animal might bolt. One who favoured a bridge showed remarkable foresight when he said numerous carriages would be detained at the crossing and in years to come the decision not to build a bridge would not only be complained of but lamented. In 1879 two young cyclists accidentally ran into the gates. The NER charged them with wilful damage but when it was learnt an offer to pay for damage had been refused, the court described the NER's conduct as disgraceful, refused costs and told the company the gates were a great nuisance and ought to be removed.

Complaints about the gates grew as road traffic increased. In 1912 a bus driver complained on one occasion 20 vehicles had been delayed for five minutes, and in the local press "Ratepayer and Passholder" thought it time the NER received notice to stop "this public nuisance." To ensure the gates were not closed to road traffic longer than necessary the signalman at Starbeck North had by 1918 instructions not to offer trains to Starbeck South box, which controlled the gates, until they were ready to start. In 1928 Harrogate Corporation complained the fire engine had been delayed at the gates for two minutes, but the LNER's only reply was that if in future notice was given of the fire engine's approach the gates would be kept open for it.

A survey taken on 5th September 1928 showed between 8.00 am and 8.00 pm the gates were closed to road traffic 144 times, causing a total delay to road users of 5 hours 1 minute and 3 seconds. Throughout the 1930s various by-pass routes were suggested but when it seemed something might be done war intervened. Another survey taken in April 1954 showed between 7.00 am and 11.00 pm, the gates were closed to road traffic for a total of 3 hours and 54 minutes. During this time 5,421 road vehicles passed over the crossing 1,230 of which were delayed. The periods the gates were closed varied from 1 to 10 minutes but it was most common for them to be closed for 3 minutes. From 7.00 am to 9.00 am the gates were closed to road traffic for periods totalling one hour. In the first five months of 1956 the "Harrogate Herald", in a campaign against the gates, published each week a different photo of the vehicles delayed. The question of a bypass was again raised but in 1958 BR announced in future delays would be less because shunting at Starbeck was to be considerably reduced. Starbeck North signalbox was closed on 7th October 1973 and Starbeck South box renamed Starbeck. In 1974 lifting barriers replaced the level crossing gates at Starbeck and Belmont.

The origins of Starbeck loco shed are obscure. There appears to have been an engine shed at Knaresborough, but not at Starbeck. In 1852 a passenger who waited at Starbeck for the last train to Leeds, which had been derailed at Northallerton, complained the stationmaster did nothing to get Leeds passengers home for two hours, except to send to Knaresborough for an engine, even though he knew its fire would have to be lit, and its crew found. The shed at Knaresborough is believed to have gone by 1875. By 1858 an engine shed had been built at Starbeck. In 1863 a short connecting line was authorised at Starbeck. This formed a triangle with existing lines and enabled trains to travel between Pannal and Knaresborough without passing through Starbeck station. By 1900, at least, the points at the Knaresborough end had been removed. The interior

Plate 14.1 One of the original eight BR Derby Lightweight DMUs, Nos. 79507/79007, comes over the level crossing into Starbeck station with a Knaresborough – Bradford Exchange via Leeds Central service. When both North and South goods yards were in operation there were frequent complaints about the delays to road traffic. The south yard closed in September 1959. J.W. Armstrong Trust.

Plate 14.2 With Starbeck shed in the background NER Worsdell design 0-8-0, No. 715 of LNER class Q5 disposes of its train in the down yard c1937. A class of 90 locomotives, this engine was allocated to Starbeck at this time, though a large number were stabled at Newport (Middlesbrough). G.Pierson collection.

of this triangle was gradually filled by the engine shed and by Stonefall sidings. On 25th November 1882 a young female pedestrian passed through a wicket gate at the level crossing at Starbeck station. After waiting for the 1.05 pm Leeds - Harrogate, via Starbeck, train to pass she began to cross the line and was killed by a southbound goods. This was the first fatality at the crossing since 1857 when a workhouse inmate had been killed by a light engine. This later incident led to the erection of a footbridge at the south end of the station. At this time Starbeck's post office was on the station's down platform and the Board of Trade recommended a pillar box be erected on the up side, so people posting letters could do so without crossing the line.

On 1st September 1890 two passengers who alighted from a returning Scarborough – Harrogate excursion at Knaresborough failed to close the carriage door properly with the result a female passenger fell out at Starbeck and was killed. The NER later paid £100 compensation to the dead girl's father. A boy fell from a train approaching Starbeck in August 1910 but suffered no more than a few bruises.

In 1882 an average of 35 passenger trains and approximately 85 goods trains and light engines, passed through Starbeck daily. There were also numerous shunting movements and Starbeck South signalbox was open day and night. In 1893, when a strike of West Riding miners created a high demand for Durham coal, complaints were made that the whistling of coal trains, which passed through Starbeck almost every hour, could be heard in almost every part of Harrogate.

Early on Sunday 29th January 1893 a Leeds - Darlington goods on restarting from Stonefall Sidings ran through buffer stops and severely damaged Starbeck South signalbox. The signalman, seeing the train approaching, jumped through the window on the other side of the box and landed without serious injury. The loco crew, who believed the points were set for the main line, escaped unhurt. A breakdown crew from Leeds arrived at about 4.00 am and found the loco eight or nine feet inside the box and the signalling mechanism twisted and smashed. By 6.00 am they had re-railed the loco and around 8.30 am were joined by a breakdown crew from York who commenced building a temporary signal box. By Monday morning trains were running as normal, the points and signals being worked from a raised platform.

Starbeck station was extended in 1898 new platform canopies also being provided at the same time. Five years later a subway replaced the footbridge and a public subscription of £60 enabled a footpath to be made along the foot of the railway embankment on the up side of the line between Belmont and Starbeck, thus providing a short cut.

The opening of the Bower Road goods yard in Harrogate had little effect on the work at Starbeck, much of which involved the transhipment of goods. The tranship shed situated in Starbeck North Yard was greatly enlarged in 1903. A problem that caused serious concern that year was the petty pilfering by railwaymen in the tranship shed. A plain-clothes policeman was put on watch and at 2.00 am one Sunday morning saw a railwayman enter a wagon, break open a barrel and steal 2 lb. of grapes. The railwayman was sacked and later fined £1 - In the same month another ex-railwayman was fined 2s for stealing two caps. The seriousness of the situation at Starbeck was explained and a warning issued that should a third offender come before the court a prison sentence would be considered.

By 1908 the NER employed approximately 510 men at Starbeck and was largely responsible for the population increasing from approximately 800 in 1889 to almost 5,000 in 1909. A branch of the Railway Mission had been established in 1888 with the first meetings held in a waiting room on Starbeck station. After a move to a converted railway stable a mission hall was built in Forest Avenue in 1909. This was extended in 1932.

On 28th February 1910 Stonefall signalbox was replaced by a new Stonefall box further south, at the end of the marshalling yard. Some new signals were installed but others dispensed with. Three points worked from the old box were in future hand worked by shunters. This meant locos at the south end of the loco shed yard had now to be signalled by hand. Also in some cases the signalman could not see when shunting was finished and if the Starbeck - Pannal line was clear or not. The shunters therefore had to inform him and for this purpose an extra telephone was installed in the up side shunters' cabin.

In September 1910 a tool van was allocated to Starbeck to deal with minor derailments. If a derailment occurred the loco foreman at Starbeck had to be informed. He then decided whether the tool van should handle it or whether the Leeds or York tool van should be sent for.

Engine whistles were often sounded to indicate to signalmen the line a driver wished to take. This sometimes led to complaints from nearby residents about excessive whistling. To keep whistling at Starbeck to a minimum bell keys were fixed to the east wall of the loco shed. When

Plate 14.3 Harrogate pilot engine, Class J77 0-6-0T, No. 68393, approaches Bog Lane bridge on 11th June 1952 with a Harrogate – Starbeck goods. At this time a number of oil companies had depots on Dragon Road with stand pipes in Harrogate goods yard accounting for the inclusion of petrol tanks in the train. Behind the fencing lies the Air Ministry aviation fuel supply depot built shortly before World War Two.
J.W. Armstrong Trust.

Plate 14.4 Starbeck station was rebuilt in 1897-8 with new platform buildings and canopies. The L.& T. branch to Knaresborough, authorised in 1848 and opened in October 1851. diverged immediately south of the level crossing. Starbeck had a goods tranship shed, extensive coal depots and cattle docks to the right of this view. All railway buildings seen in this view, apart from the extant signal box, were demolished in the early 1970s.
K.L. Taylor collection.

operated they rang a bell in Starbeck South signalbox telling the signalman the line the driver wanted.

The number of wagons dealt with at Starbeck in 1913 was 381,334. By 1925 the number had increased to 413,433. The North Yard could accommodate 169 wagons and Stonefall sidings 759 wagons, 262 on the up side and 497 on the down. By 1927 it was common for the up side to be full and for wagons to have to stand on the Starbeck - Pannal line, causing delays. Also by 1927 the number of passenger trains passing through Starbeck each weekday had increased from 64, in 1913, to 84 and it was difficult to find a path through the station for goods trains and pilot trips. It was therefore decided to provide eight new sidings at Stonefall at a cost of £2,387.

In 1929 the Royal Agricultural Show was held in Harrogate. To handle goods traffic generated by this show wooden platforms were erected in Stonefall sidings.

In the 1920s Sentinel steam railcars were allocated to Starbeck shed to work local passenger services. The new Sentinel steam railcar 244 "True Briton" was introduced on the Harrogate - Knaresborough service on 6th April 1928. Whilst being shunted in Starbeck shed yard in August 1928 it ran away. The fireman gave chase but was crushed to death between the car and the shed wall as he tried to climb abroad. In August 1933 one roster involved a Sentinel car leaving Starbeck shed for Knaresborough at 5.25 am. At 5.43 am it began one of 24 return trips between Knaresborough and Harrogate, as well as an additional Harrogate - Starbeck return trip, and returned to the shed at 10.55 pm. On Saturdays it made 22 return trips between Knaresborough and Harrogate and, as well as the additional Harrogate – Starbeck return trip, worked the 9.00 pm Harrogate - Wetherby and return. Also, instead of returning to the shed at 10.55 pm, it left Harrogate at 11.05 pm for Melmerby and then ran empty back to Starbeck, arriving at 12.09 am. At one time Starbeck also had a Class Y3, 0-4-0T, Sentinel shunter which was frequently to be seen at Ripon.

In June 1935 a Sentinel railcar was brought safely into Starbeck station by the fireman after the driver had died at the controls after leaving Knaresborough. The last Sentinel Car allocated to Starbeck, 2147 "Woodpecker", was withdrawn from the shed in January 1947.

During an enginemen's strike in 1867 the tradesmen and hotel proprietors of Harrogate hoped the strike would soon be settled for they were almost entirely dependent on the railway for the supply of goods. When the first national railway strike occurred, in 1911, goods were brought into Harrogate by road. This caused the local press to predict that in any future strike the motor car would play a prominent part in alleviating any distress caused by lack of food. By the 1930s the railways were faced not only with increased competition from the roads but also the Depression. In 1932 Harrogate Corporation decided in future coal and coke for its electricity works would be brought from Pontefract by road instead of rail. This would save almost £1,000 a year in transport costs. The competition from roads was to a large extent unfair because the railways were bound by antiquated laws. This led them to start the "Square Deal" campaign by which they hoped to influence public opinion and bring about a change in the law. In the meantime they continued to seek economies, which led some to believe Starbeck shed and yards might close. They therefore urged Harrogatonians to support the "Square Deal" campaign because 75% of Starbeck's population depended, either directly or indirectly, on the railway for their livelihood. Unfortunately the campaign, which began in 1938, never fully developed because of the war.

During week ending 11th July 1943 9,630 wagons were detached at Stonefall sidings, but during week ending 6 July 1947 the number was only 4,522. In 1948 there was still enough work to keep five pilot locos employed, but by 1952 falling traffic and more economical working had reduce the number to two. Transhipping in the North Yard ceased in 1950.

The cleaning of some carriages was carried out at Stonefall sidings. In April 1949 the empty stock of the 10.15 am from Kings Cross had been placed in quarantine there after the BBC had broadcast a warning that a passenger travelling by this train was thought to have smallpox.

Stonefall signalbox closed on 7th October 1951 following closure of the Pannal - Starbeck line. It was dismantled and re-erected as Widdrington North-on the ECML between Newcastle and Berwick. In 1953 plans were made to rebuild Starbeck loco shed. The roof was replaced but the shed's length reduced from approximately 370 to 270 feet. Plans to increase the shed's width so three roads instead of two would be under cover were not carried out.

ASLEF, the footplatemen's union, went on strike in June 1955. On 11th June 22 drivers and 26 firemen and cleaners were on strike at Starbeck. Most of the shed's footplatemen however belonged to the NUR and 61 drivers and 57 firemen and cleaners remained at work.

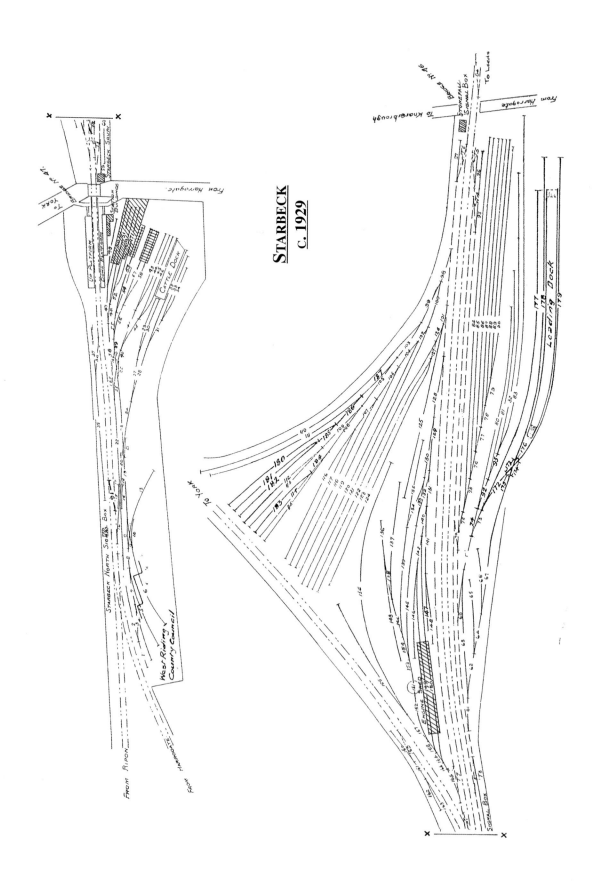

STARBECK
C. 1929

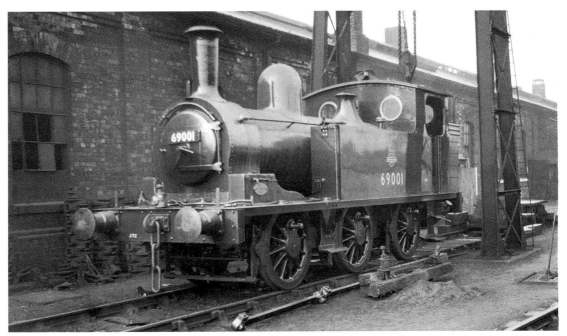

Plate 14.6   Newly built by Darlington Works this BR built class J72 0-6-0 tank engine has come to grief en route to its new home in Hull with over-heated bearings. On 12th October 1949 it is standing under the shear legs at the rear of Starbeck shed prior to being lifted - both sets of coupling rods have been taken down for this purpose.   G.Pierson collection.

Plate 14.7   This view of the engine shed and yard taken on 24th July 1938 gives some impression of how long the shed was – it had been extended on at least four occasions. The engines seen stabled on this occasion were : - 1464, 2020, 1245, 1483, 2107, 1723, 1241, 954, 408, 1788, 276, 2108, 712, 1098, 2012.   B.Roberts/J.A.Peden collection

Chapter 15

SOME PROPOSED RAILWAYS AND TRAMWAYS

If all Knaresborough people had been gifted with the foresight of Mother Shipton, their town's famous prophetess, Knaresborough might have become the birthplace of the world's first steam worked public railway. In 1802 the building of a railway, about 1½ miles long from Knaresborough to Cold Keld, near Scriven, was considered. This would have joined a proposed canal to Ellenthorpe Shoals, near Boroughbridge, where another canal, to the Tees, was proposed. Cheap Durham coal would then have been available in Knaresborough but when the proposal for this latter canal came to nothing the scheme could not gain sufficient support.

In 1818 Thomas Telford made a survey for a canal to provide Knaresborough with cheap coal from the West Riding. He reported there were two routes a canal might take, one from the Ouse, a mile below Union Lock, another from the Wharfe, about a mile above Tadcaster. Unfortunately the number of locks made the cost of either canal prohibitive. It was therefore suggested a canal be built from Acaster Selby on the Ouse, to Ribston Green, on the Crimple, and linked to Knaresborough by a double track railway at an estimated cost of £92,864. The canal scheme was abandoned when it was discovered a railway could be laid from Acaster Selby to Knaresborough for about £60,000 and continued to Pateley Bridge, as a single line, for an additional £38,830. Later, to avoid tolls on the Ouse above the mouth of the Wharfe, Bolton Percy replaced Acaster Selby as the proposed eastern terminus. The railway was expected to reduce the price of coal in Knaresborough, and the cost of transporting flax, the spinning of which was Knaresborough's main industry, by about one third. A few passengers were expected, and it was thought steam locomotives might be used, but the promoters, not having employed an engineer familiar with these machines, could say nothing further at that time. Unfortunately when made public, in 1820, the scheme could not gain sufficient support and five years later the Stockton and Darlington Railway became the first steam worked public railway in the world.

The Northern Counties Union Railway proposed a line from Thirsk to the Lancaster & Carlisle Railway near Penrith in 1846 including a branch from Melmerby to join this line near Bedale. The lines were never completed but for 2½ miles north of Melmerby the L & T used the old workings when building its Stockton extension.

In 1879 a new company proposed a line from Leeds to Harrogate, via Roundhay Park and Kirkby Overblow, but this came to nothing. A 1901 scheme for a 3 ft gauge tramway from Littlethorpe to Kirkby Malzeard and a scheme for a 3 ft 6 in gauge tramway from Ripon to Studley Royal also came to nothing. Knaresborough Urban District Council proposed a light railway between Knaresborough and Harrogate in 1898 but this was opposed by Harrogate Corporation. Harrogate Corporation proposed its own tramway in 1902. Trams were proposed to run from Harrogate to Bilton, New Park, Oatlands, Starbeck and Knaresborough. This was welcomed by Knaresborough residents who thought it might induce the NER to improve services and reduce fares between Knaresborough and Harrogate. Harrogate Corporation however only proposed the tramway to prevent a private company building one which, in the Corporation's opinion, would destroy the peace of the town. The proposed Harrogate - Knaresborough route was cut back so it terminated not in Knaresborough Market Place, as originally planned, but at the town boundary, mid-way between Starbeck and Knaresborough, and eventually the entire scheme was abandoned.

1901 saw the completion of the doubling the lines between Northallerton and Melmerby and between Wetherby and Cross Gates, and the building of a new south-west curve at Wetherby. The previous year they had drawn up plans for a line approximately 5¼ miles long from Belmont to join the Harrogate - Church Fenton line between Spofforth and Wetherby. The estimated cost of this new line was £141,700. It would have called for two viaducts. One 750 feet long and 63 feet high would have crossed the Harrogate - Wetherby road near Plompton Rocks, the other, 3 miles from Belmont, would have been 540 feet long and 42 feet high. No stations or level crossings were planned on the line whose gradients would have been less steep than those between Bilton and Wetherby. The line, which was never built, would have enabled goods trains to avoid both the congestion at Harrogate station and at Holbeck.

In 1907 a new company proposed a railway from Sheffield to Newcastle, via Bradford, Otley and Harrogate. The first route proposed approached Harrogate through a tunnel under Harlow Hill before reaching a station near Jennyfield. Because it would cut through several mineral springs it was opposed by Harrogate Corporation, who sent the promoters a map showing all the mineral springs in the area, and by August 1907 a revised route had been submitted. This approached Harrogate to the west of the Leeds - Harrogate line, under which it was to pass near the old Brunswick Tunnel. The new line would then have run parallel to the NER across the Stray but, despite being only four feet lower, would have run in a tunnel because the Corporation would not allow a second cutting across the Stray. It would have emerged opposite the NER station, where the new company planned their own station. From here the line would have entered another tunnel and crossed under the NER line, between the goods yard and Dragon Jct., before emerging and proceeding north. The line however never grew to be more than a proposal and as such was soon abandoned.

Plate 15.1 Before working the afternoon 16.50 London Kings Cross train one of the East Coast routes famous Class 55 Deltics, No. 55016, 'The Gordon Highlander' lies in the remaining south end bay platform at Harrogate prior to rejoining its train during July 1975. Deltics remained regular visitors to Harrogate, particularly on the evening 17.05 Yorkshire Pullman from London. Deltic hauled services to Harrogate ceased with the introduction of HSTs in 1978. J.H. Williamson

Plate 15.2 LNER Class D49/2, No. 366, 'The Oakley' stands with a train of Gresley design Tourist stock outside Starbeck shed in 1936. Tourist stock was introduced in an effort to encourage excusion traffic and with that in mind the coaches were painted cream and green following contemporary motor coach colour schemes instead of the usual LNER livery of varnished teak. The second and third vehicles are an articulated twin-set open third. The matching leading brake third and Buffet car further down the train complete the tourist coach designs introduced c1933-9. RAS Marketing.

A BRIEF CHRONOLOGY OF HARROGATE'S RAILWAYS.

17th June 1847	Pilmoor - Boroughbridge branch opened
10th August 1847	Church Fenton - Spofforth section of YNMR line opened
5th January 1848	Thirsk - Ripon section of L & T line opened to goods traffic
1st June 1848	Thirsk - Ripon section of L & T line opened to passenger traffic
20th July 1848	Spofforth - Harrogate section of YNMR line opened.
13th September 1848	Ripon - Weeton section of L & T line opened.
30th October 1848	E & WYJR's York - Knaresborough line opened as far as Haya Park Lane, Knaresborough
9th July 1849	Leeds & Thirsk Railway opened throughout.
21st July 1851	Haya Park Lane - Knaresborough section of E & WYJR opened.
18th August 1851	Knaresborough - Starbeck line opened.
15th May 1852	Melmerby - Stockton line opened to goods traffic
2nd June 1852	Melmerby - Stockton line opened to passenger traffic.
31st July 1854	The York & North Midland Railway, the York Newcastle & Berwick Railway and the Leeds Northern Railway amalgamate to form the North Eastern Railway
1st May 1862	Pateley Bridge branch opened
1st August 1862	Harrogate station opened. Also new lines linking the L & T to the YNMR line with the Harrogate - Church Fenton line. Brunswick station closed to passengers.
1st February 1865	Arthington - Otley line opened
1st August 1865	Otley - Ilkley line opened.
1st April 1875	Knaresborough - Boroughbridge line opened
9th June 1875	Masham branch opened
1st May 1876	Cross Gates - Wetherby line opened
1st July 1902	New Wetherby station opened.
11th September 1907	Nidd Valley Light Railway opened
c1908	Harrogate Gas Works Railway opened
1st January 1923	Railways grouped into four large companies. The North Eastern Railway becomes part of the London & North Eastern Railway.
31st December 1929	Passenger service withdrawn from the Nidd Valley Light Railway
1st January 1931	Passenger service withdrawn from the Masham branch
c1936	Nidd Valley Light Railway closed completely
1st January 1948	Railways nationalised.
25th September 1950	Passenger service withdrawn from the Boroughbridge branch
31st March 1951	Passenger service withdrawn from the Pateley Bridge branch.
7th October 1951	Pannal Jct. - Starbeck line officially closed
October 1956	Harrogate Gas Works Railway closed
25th February 1957	Harrogate - Bradford Forster Square service withdrawn
13th September 1959	Melmerby - Thirsk line closed completely
13th September 1959	Starbeck shed and marshalling yard closed.
11th November 1963	Masham branch closed completely
6th January 1964	Passenger services to Wetherby withdrawn. Crimple - Wetherby line closes completely.
6th October 1964	Boroughbridge branch closed completely
31st October 1964	Pateley Bridge branch closed completely.
22nd March 1965	Passenger service withdrawn from the Arthington - Otley line. Arthington station closed.
5th July 1965	Arthington - Otley Line closed completely
4th April 1966	Wetherby closed to goods traffic.
30th November 1966	Goods traffic withdrawn from Tadcaster. The last station on the Wetherby lines with a goods service.
6th March 1967	Passenger service withdrawn from the Harrogate - Northallerton line.
9th October 1969	Last goods train on Starbeck - Northallerton line.
July 1984	Harrogate Goods Yard closed

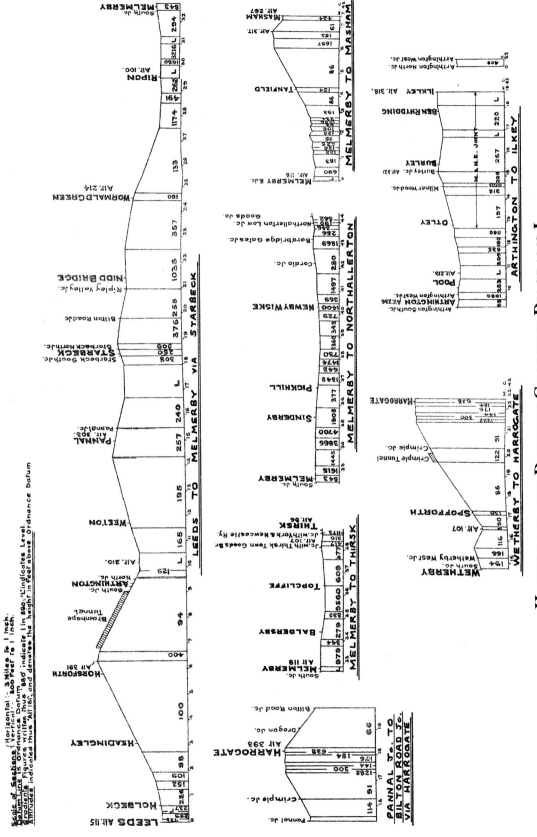

HARROGATE AND DISTRICT GRADIENT DIAGRAMS I

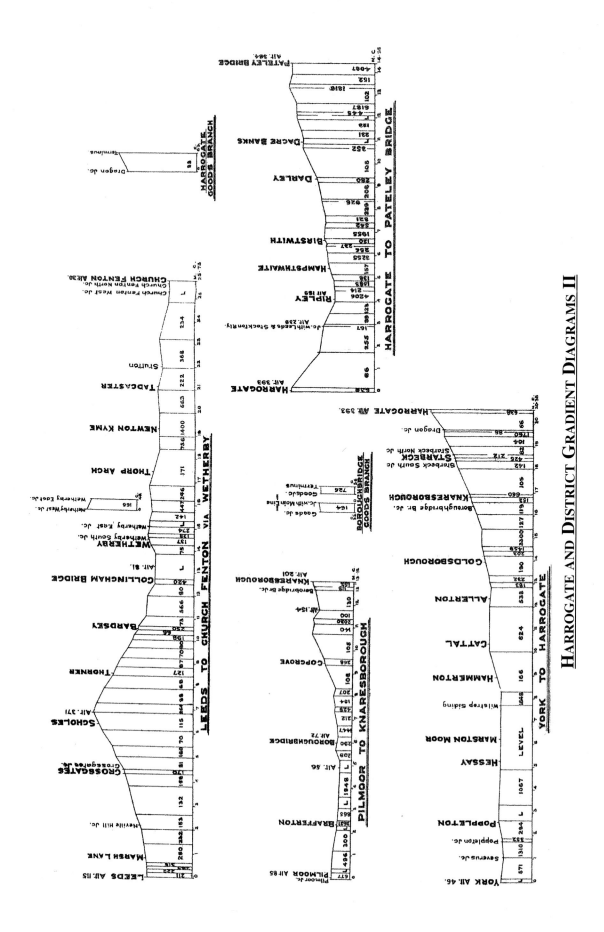

HARROGATE AND DISTRICT GRADIENT DIAGRAMS II

110

one driver if the two spotless locos were new, and why two were needed. She was informed they were not new and that her train was a very heavy one. After visiting Goldsborough in 1924 the Queen left in a royal saloon attached to an ordinary Harrogate - York passenger train.

During the Second World War a rail connected cold storage depot was opened at Goldsborough. For this the station received a new signalbox which opened on 10th November 1942. In 1969 a bridge carrying the Harrogate - York road over the railway replaced the level crossing and also later enabled the signalbox to be closed in February 1971.

At Wilstrop, between Hammerton and Marston Moor, wooden platforms enabled locals to use trains on market days. There was also a small covered siding for goods traffic. Passenger trains ceased to call from 1st May 1931 but the goods siding remained in use until 4th May 1964.

Until 1951 a shuttle service ran between Harrogate and Knaresborough. When it was withdrawn railwaymen and local politicians complained to the British Transport Commission, but were told before the war the Harrogate - Knaresborough service had run at a loss with an average of only 18 passengers on each train, less than one third the seating capacity of the Sentinel cars that had been used.

On 18th August 1958 diesel railcars were introduced on the Harrogate - York service. For a while the 3.40 pm, Saturdays excepted, and the 5.14 pm from Harrogate, and the 12.24 pm and 8.30 pm from York, remained steam hauled, but by 5th January 1959 all passenger services on

MARSTON MOOR

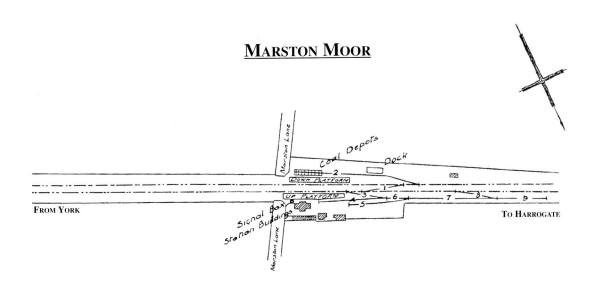

the line were worked by railcars. Goldsborough, Hopperton, Marston Moor and Hessay stations, however, had little chance to benefit from the diesels as they closed to passengers from 15th September 1958. Until October 1896 Marston Moor had been called Marston and until October 1925 Hopperton was known as Allerton. By June 1965, with the exception of Starbeck and Harrogate, goods traffic had been withdrawn from all the stations on the line. A private siding to a military depot at Hessay remained in use until 1995.

Under the Beeching plan withdrawal of passenger services from the Harrogate – York line was to have taken place from 30th November 1964 but was postponed following 337 objections. The passenger service between Harrogate and Northallerton was also proposed for closure. This meant if both routes closed Harrogate would have no rail access to the North, except via the roundabout route via Leeds. On 20th September 1966 consent to the withdrawal of passenger services between Harrogate and York was refused.

In summer 1961 Sundays trains were reintroduced between Harrogate and York for the first time since before the war, but a Sunday service in winter was not provided until 1967, after the withdrawal of trains between Harrogate and Northallerton, via Ripon. On 15th June 1969 conductor guards were introduced on York - Harrogate - Leeds trains and all intermediate stations, except Harrogate, became unstaffed. Another economy measure was the reduction to single line in 1973 of the Knaresborough - Cattal and Hammerton – Poppleton sections of line. It was also proposed to single the line between Starbeck and Harrogate but this was not proceeded with.

There have been a number of accidents on the line. During construction of the line in September 1847 a large number of man were excavating a cutting at Kirk Hammerton when a large quantity of earth fell on them. They were dug out but three were so badly injured it was reported they were not expected to recover. In 1856 the stationmaster at Hopperton was killed in a shunting accident at the station, and on 29th October 1866 two passengers were injured when an excursion train brushed a derailed wagon at Knaresborough. The door and grab handles were torn off about 17 carriages and many windows broken.

In 1864 a youth was caught placing iron rail chairs on the line near Knaresborough, and in 1867 a 12 year old boy was caught doing the same between Hammerton and Marston Moor.

One man was killed, and another severely injured, on 12th August 1874 when a light engine travelling to Starbeck struck their cart on the level crossing at Goldsborough. The Goldsborough stationmaster, who had charge of the gates, had cleared the signals for the engine before he closed the gates to road traffic, and so allowed the cart onto the line. He won the public's sympathy when it was learnt the men in the cart had been drinking and had ignored his warning to stop. The coroner's jury thought the duties at Goldsborough too much for one man. Nevertheless the stationmaster was found guilty of manslaughter and sentenced to two month's imprisonment without hard labour.

On 16th August 1875 while repairs were made to the bridge over the Nidd near Hammerton trains were worked across on a single line. As the 12.15 pm Harrogate - York was passing over temporary points the Wilstrop signalman moved them, causing a carriage to fall onto its side crushing a female passenger. In January 1883, Mrs Sadler, the wife of the landlord of the "Three Horse Shoes" at Kirk Hammerton, was killed by a train whilst using Hammerton station's level crossing.

In 1882 a Staveley innkeeper was killed at Knaresborough station. He had passed through a level crossing gate, as a porter was about to close it. While walking the short distance to the platform he was struck by a Knaresborough - Boroughbridge train.

Two platelayers, working on the line between Dragon Jct. and Starbeck, were killed on 6th May 1914 when they stepped out of the way of a Harrogate bound goods into the path of a Harrogate - Leeds, via Starbeck, train they failed to see because of a curve in the line. The signalman at Belmont was sacked in July 1852 after a train ran through the level crossing gates. The gates were smashed again on February 1910 when 3.10 pm Harrogate - York autocar ran through them.

In January 1931 a motor van was completely smashed, and its wreckage scattered along the line, after it crashed through the gates at Hopperton and was struck by the 8.25 am Harrogate - York passenger train. The van's load of films caught fire and trailed along the train scorching the carriage sides. No one was hurt, although the loco, Class D23, 4-4-0, No. 328, was derailed. Another accident happened to the same train at Hopperton on 22nd July 1933. Part of the loco's valve gear came loose and damaged the track for three-quarters of a mile. During thick fog on 28th March 1934 a northbound lorry ran through the gates at Hopperton and was struck by a York - Harrogate train. The lorry was swept onto the front of the loco, knocking over a gatepost, a station lamp and hitting the down side waiting room, five feet from the platform edge. After knocking over some railings the lorry, by this time on fire, fell off. The train continued for 600 yards, on greasy rails, before it stopped. The lorry driver, who had jumped clear, was unhurt but all signals in the vicinity were put out of action.

When a northbound lorry skidded through the gates on the down side on a foggy day in January 1949 the Hopperton stationmaster shouted to the driver to continue to smash through the gates on the up side. This saved the lorry from being hit by the 10.10 am from York which was slowing to stop at the station. In the previous seven weeks three lorries had crashed through the gates. One had pushed a gate into the path of a train, which had carried it some distance before stopping. Accidents of this nature ceased when a bridge carrying the A1 over the railway was built to replace the level crossing in 1962. However on a foggy 31st August 1974 the 8.12 am York - Harrogate killed eight cows being herded across the line at this point, and in April 1988 train services were disrupted when a lorry ran through the parapet of the bridge. Rubble fell onto the line and the lorry was left perched precariously above the line. Fortunately no train was passing at the time. The A1 has since been widened and in 1995 another bridge was provided.

On 20th May 1935 a ballast train struck a van on an occupation crossing near Knaresborough. The van driver jumped clear, but his vehicle was carried on the front of the loco towards Goldsborough for 382 yards before it hit a signalpost and fell off.

Plate 7.5 Hammerton station had a distinctive sloping roof waiting shed and goods store on the down platform. Under the canopy of the up side the otherwise open lever frame is hidden by a small hut – a feature of many minor North Eastern stations. D.J. Williamson collection.

Plate 7.6 The small station Hessay of closed on 15th September 1958, the main road to York with its bus service probably being more attractive and convenient to the local residents. Hessay and Hammerton have architectural similarities but both are smaller structures than the other stations on the line. D.J. Williamson.

McKenzie, unfortunately, discovered he had left his wallet at home. Bass therefore lent him £3. Later when Bass contacted the station site he was told they had never heard of McKenzie. Needless to say McKenzie was never heard of again.

In response to a request from Harrogate and York residents for an express service between the two places the NER announced that a daily express train, stopping en route only at Knaresborough, would be introduced from 1st May 1893. It would leave Harrogate at 8.25 am and arrive in York at 9.00 am. In the opposite direction York would be departed at 4.45 pm and Harrogate reached at 5.20 pm. Following complaints that 4.45 pm was too early for businessmen still at work the time was altered to 5.40 pm, with arrival in Harrogate at 6.10 pm. In addition there were, in August 1893, only six trains per weekday in each direction between Harrogate and York, and no Sunday service. The average journey time was 55 minutes.

In the same year the NER refused to reduce the price of third class quarterly season tickets from Knaresborough to Harrogate after passengers complained such tickets cost £1 2s 6d, 3s 6d more than such tickets from Horsforth to Leeds, a journey 2 miles longer.

The local press complained in 1902 that almost weekly complaints were made about spitting in Harrogate and Knaresborough trains whose floors were being converted into spittoons. In 1903 there were complaints about overcrowding, and following alterations to the timetable, that the 5.05 pm and 5.08 pm from York to Harrogate left too early for businessmen. It was thought ridiculous to have two trains leave within three minutes of each other, especially as the next, previously the 5.55 pm, did not now leave until 6.25 pm, and was often delayed awaiting late running connections. Two years later Harrogate Traders Association asked for a train from Harrogate to York between 12.50 pm and 4.40 pm because, except on Knaresborough market day, there were none between those times. They also asked for better connections at York.

From 2 July 1906 a steam autocar was introduced on the Harrogate - York line to augment the ordinary service. These trains ran as follows:

	PM	PM
York dep.	12.15	2.30
Harrogate arr.	12.52	3.05
Harrogate dep	1.20	3.15
York arr.	1.56	3.48

The 12.15 pm from York stopped at Poppleton, and also at Knaresborough to set down. The 1.20 pm from Harrogate stopped to take up at Knaresborough, otherwise all four trains ran non - stop. In December 1906 trains were stranded in snow drifts between Dragon Jct. and Starbeck North, and at Goldsborough, consequently trains between Harrogate and York were diverted via Bilton, Starbeck and Boroughbridge.

The NER were often asked to provide a Sunday service between Harrogate and York, if only to allow passengers to worship in York Minster, but they refused, stating in 1910 that the running of just one train between the two places on the Sabbath would require 62 extra men.

On Knaresborough Carnival Day in 1913 a continuous char-a-banc service was run between Harrogate and Knaresborough as well as a train service. That day 6,440 tickets were collected from railway passengers at Knaresborough.

During the first national railway strike in 1911 all 29 railwaymen employed at Knaresborough remained at work. Afterwards each received 14s 8d from a fund set up by grateful residents. The stationmaster, J Dobson, distributed his share amongst his men. He retired in 1930 after 51 years on the railway, during which time he never missed a day through illness.

When Mr W G Lawson, stationmaster at Hammerton, transferred to Wykeham in 1912 the residents of Kirk Hammerton and Nun Monkton presented him with an illuminated address and a purse of gold while the residents of Green Hammerton presented him with a marble and bronze clock.

On 8 December 1923 the NER Cottage Homes and Benefit Fund opened five houses at Knaresborough. These were named "Stevenson Place" after Arthur Stevenson, the Fund's Chairman and the NER's Estate Agent.

In 1923 King George V and Prince George arrived at Goldsborough station to attend a christening at Goldsborough Church. Queen Mary arrived by road but joined her husband, the King, for the return to London. The ex LNWR Royal Train of ten coaches was brought empty from York by a LNER loco, newly painted black. This was exchanged at Goldsborough for two ex Midland Railway locos, which were to haul the train to St Pancras, via York. The Queen asked

Pannal signal box was built when block signalling was introduced to the Leeds Northern in
1873. The box took over the functions of Pannal
Junction when that box closed in 1927 and motor
operated points were installed remotely controlled
from Pannal Station. Note the NER milepost to
the left. With the closure of the line to Starbeck
and withdrawal of goods facilities Pannal signal
box was closed in March 1968.
John Bateman/D.J. Williamson collection.

The signal box at Bardsey was situated at the top
of an embankment resulting in the construction of
a wooden structure to accommodate the lever
frame.   Bardsey box closed on 2nd August 1965
though the station lost its passenger and goods
services on 6th January 1964.
R.T.H.Platt/D.J. Williamson collection.

Starbeck South signal box oversees the busy level
crossing on the main road through Starbeck to
Knaresborough. In the heyday of the railway at
Starbeck the frequent procession of through goods
trains and movements between the freight yards to
the north and south of the crossing brought
repeated lengthy hold-ups to road traffic.
Starbeck South controlled the junction between
the Knaresborough branch and the Leeds
Northern plus connections to the south yard
and engine shed.
D.J. Williamson.

A BR Derby Lightweight DMU stands at the up platform at Knaresborough having terminated with a working from Leeds. A prominent BR(NE) pattern bracket signal is situated in front of the main station buildings. Much the same scene can be viewed today – indeed the water tank and railings above the tunnel portal have been restored with the help of grants from the Railway Heritage Trust. The main station buildings of 1865, rebuilt in 1890, have also benefited from the grant aid enabling repainting and also the reglazing of the canopy. The station is unmanned apart from the signalman. The station building now houses a number of small businesses.   D.J. Williamson collection.

Double headed LNER Gresley class D49 4-4-0s, Nos. 62749 'The Cottesmore' and 62736 'The Bramham Moor' stand at platform 4 on an up express sometime in the 1950's.   D.J. Williamson collection.